SURVIVING THE STORM

The New Geopolitics of Energy

Windsor Energy Group

Surviving the Storm
The New Geopolitics of Energy

Published by
Medina Publishing Ltd
310 Ewell Road
Surbiton
Surrey KT6 7AL
www.medinapublishing.com

Copyright © Windsor Energy Group 2015
All contributors retain individual copyright

ISBN: 978-1-909339-52-1

CIP Data: A catalogue record for this book is available from the British Library

Printed and Bound in Great Britain by TJ International Ltd.

All rights reserved. No part of this publication may be reproduced, stored in a retrieval system, or transmitted in any form or by any means, electronic, mechanical, photocopying, recording, or otherwise, without the prior permission of the copyright owners.

SURVIVING THE STORM

The New Geopolitics of Energy

conceived and co-ordinated by Paul Tempest
photographs by Cathy Arnold

Windsor Energy Group

CONTENTS

Foreword	HE Khaled Al-Duwaisan	vii
Preface		ix
Prologue	The Gathering Storm: Paul Tempest	1
Chapter One	Plenty of Clean Energy: Lord Howell	13
Chapter Two	Energy Imbroglio: Lord Howell	19
Chapter Three	US Energy Policy: Dr Herman Franssen	35
Chapter Four	China's Energy Dynamics: Andrew Leung	43
Chapter Five	Japan and Asia – Ways Forward: Tatsuo Masuda	47
Chapter Six	The Legacy of Fossil Fuels: Lord Oxburgh	51
Postscript	Windsor Castle Annual Consultation 2014: Ian Walker	55
Conclusions	The New Geopolitics of Energy – Avoiding Catastrophe	61

Tables

1	Primary Energy Consumption	5
	Oil, Gas, Coal Consumption	5
	Nuclear, Hydro, Alternatives	6
2	Proved Energy Reserves – Oil, Gas, Coal	8
3	International Trade in Global Oil – Exports, Imports	9
Annex	Windsor Energy Group – Members and Background	67

بعد العاصفة السلامة

Ba'ad al aasifa, as-salaama
After the storm comes the peace

While discussing the scope and title of this book in 2013, HE Khalid Al-Mansouri, then Qatar Ambassador to the UK, presented us with his version of the title in Arabic. The Windsor Energy Group would like to express its appreciation of this gesture and also our most sincere thanks for his lively and enthusiastic support throughout the years of his distinguished appointment in London.

FOREWORD

by HE Khaled Al-Duwaisan

Diplomacy and Global Energy

The security of an ample long-term supply of energy reaching an ever-expanding global population is essential for human health and welfare and indeed for human survival. The continuing momentum of increases in energy supply is also essential for environmental protection and for the generation of new energy technology. This depends on adequate long-term investment and the progressive reduction of conflict achieved by global understanding of the need, aided by high levels of diplomatic expediency. There is no question of choice here. Somehow we have to surmount the proliferating obstacles of political confrontation, economic impoverishment, increasing volatility in the markets and the social risk of upheaval and anarchy. In this highly integrated world, we are all inter-dependent and we are all therefore vulnerable to conflagrations elsewhere, to the rapidly shifting patterns of international commercial activity and trade and to damage inflicted by a changing climate or by pollution of our atmosphere, fresh water, food and fishery sources.

Today, new exploration and production technology and improved systems of energy transportation and end-use offer solutions unheard of even a decade ago provided they can be applied rapidly and effectively worldwide. Diplomatic channels and improved telecommunications have also evolved rapidly to serve the cause of peace and global economic welfare.

These are the issues addressed in March each year by the Windsor Energy Group in its Annual Consultations in Windsor Castle since 2003.

I have been involved with the Windsor Energy Group since its inaugural dinner which was convened by its first Chairman, Sir David Gore-Booth in the Athenæum in 2000. Each year its activities have included several hosted in the Kuwait Embassy or residence. I have chaired ten of the twelve annual Ambassadors Dinners and Briefings held in Windsor Castle as well as participating in many other Windsor Energy Group activities.

This volume aims to give a thumb-nail overview of where we think the problems and opportunities lie today. They draw primarily on the reports of the Annual 3-day Consultations held in Windsor Castle since 2003 and on the programme of briefings open to the 170 or so Ambassadors and Commonwealth High Commissioners representing their country in London at any one time. Other activities involve the leading energy companies. Overseas briefings have been held at intervals in Houston, Qatar, Kuwait, Almaty, Gdansk and in the European Parliament, as well as in Berlin, Vilnius and Istanbul.

The Windsor Energy Group aims primarily to sustain relations between governments and the leading international and national energy companies. Only through human enterprise and human energy can we succeed. This is why well-informed diplomacy is so important.

Khaled Al-Duwaisan
Ambassador of Kuwait
Dean of the Diplomatic Corps

London, January 2015

PREFACE

The Windsor Energy Group (WEG) was founded in London in 2000 to provide high-level briefing and other services to London ambassadors and their governments on the current geopolitics of energy and related issues. Its aim is to help build firm bridges between the multinational energy companies, national energy corporations and their governments worldwide. HE Khaled Al-Duwaisan, Ambassador of Kuwait and Dean of the London Diplomatic Corps attended the founding dinner in the Athenæum and has been a most valued member and active supporter to this day.

The first WEG Chairman was the late Sir David Gore-Booth KCMG KCVO. Lord Howell of Guildford PC took over as Chairman in 2005/6 and remains in the position. Others involved from the outset include Paul Tempest, Executive Director/CEO until 2009 and Ian Walker who succeeded him. For details of the International Steering Panel and further background, see the Annex on page 67.

Since 2003, WEG has convened each March for three days inside Windsor Castle by courtesy of HM the Queen and invitation of HRH Prince Philip, Duke of Edinburgh. About 25 invited guests from around the world are joined by 20-25 current Ambassadors and High Commissioners for briefing in the Dungeon and dinner in the Vicars' Hall (which was completed 1415). Since 2010, a full report of these consultations has been published in the monthly *Geopolitics of Energy* founded in 1979 in Washington DC by Melvin A Conant and published since 1993 by the Canadian Energy Research Institute, Calgary. *An Enduring Friendship – 400 years of Anglo-Gulf Relations*, the first book in this WEG series, was published in 2006. Notable annual reports included *The Long Shadow of Iraq* (2003), *Rising Global Uncertainty* (2006) and *A Big Shock is Coming* (2007).

Several major WEG gatherings have been held in USA c/o the Federal Reserve Board (Houston) as well as in Tokyo, Berlin, the European Parliament, Istanbul, Vilnius, Kazakhstan (Almaty) and Gdansk, with WEG participation in national events in China, India, Qatar and Kuwait. London/UK seminars have been held for Saudi Arabia, Iceland, Poland and Russia as well as, most recently, for the Ambassador of Japan and for the High Commissioners of Australia, which will be followed by India.

This volume aims to provide food for thought for the next year of consultations and meetings and as briefing for our sponsors, ambassadors, high commissioners and young staff. In 2015 WEG will be focussing on the major challenges facing global energy markets and the "trilemma" of trying to balance energy security, energy affordability and climate change without long-term damage to human health or the global environment. Preserving the momentum of energy investment, exploration and development and accelerating the implementation of much new technology is essential.

Global politics and global energy are closely interlinked, like a DNA spiral helix. Growing unrest in major energy exporting countries deserves continuous careful analysis and assessment, while the needs of non-OECD countries, already consuming much more global primary energy than the OECD countries, have to be addressed and met with care and sensitivity. New energy-specific international institutions will be needed to force the pace of this transition.

WEG's three sister organisations, which emerged from the WEG annual consultations at Windsor will all be active. The Global Nuclear Initiative that monitors the challenges facing existing and new-build nuclear is chaired by Lady Judge, chair emeritus of the UK Atomic Energy Authority. Lord Oxburgh of Liverpool, chair of the Carbon Capture and Storage Association chairs the Network for Energy Technology. Carole Nakhle, an energy adviser to the IFC and World Bank, chairs Access for Women in Energy.

PROLOGUE
The Gathering Storm
Paul Tempest

No one on this planet knows, of course, what the future will bring and those who claim to know are all either fools, self-appointed bigots, weirdos, political manipulators (some well-meaning), or outright liars. Clever economists and other soothsayers come in two categories. First, a few really valuable people who know that they do not know and second, a larger number who do not know that they do not know. For the rest of us, more humble, toiling in the field of energy economics, it is more a patient search through the numbers (and views of the key states, alliances and personalities involved) in search of an optimum balance of cost and long-term benefit against a tumultuous background of volatile markets, constantly improving new technology and political surprise.

In ensuring adequate energy worldwide to meet the needs of a growing global population and uncertain climate, we are talking not about the two decades ahead, but the next fifty years at least. Investment today, for example, in exploration, production, processing, transportation and distribution of hydrocarbons will, in all probability, continue to provide the bulk of those energy needs. This is no small matter. Investment in energy has to be financed, mobilised and sustained on a continuing and expanding basis; it is highly dependent on the efficient application of new technology worldwide and the rapid replacement of all that is old, inefficient and obsolete. Above all, it depends on a high level of international co-operation and shared goodwill and a global consensus that such efforts are essential for sustainable global prosperity and, indeed ultimately, for human survival.

The Gathering Storm

According to our informal Windsor Energy Group index of global goodwill, the geopolitical obstacles to international trade and development have again begun to multiply alarmingly. There may be some serious trouble ahead.

In Europe the dangers of being denied, or even threatened temporarily by a denial of oil and gas imports from Russia already colour the anxieties of the 28 members of the European Union with the fear of a widespread slowdown in the manufacturing industry and economic activity. If investment plans continue to be put on hold and Western sanctions begin to bite more deeply, Russian responses will sharpen. China will probably be drawn into the confrontation and will be affected by it. Among the smaller and weaker EU members in the East, there may be panic if electricity outages, freezing homes and schools and shortages of transportation fuels begin cumulatively to sap confidence. Some of the most exposed and weaker EU members may then seek to conclude their own new Russian supply contracts with all the escalation of import cost, increased debt and erosion of trade competitiveness implied. As well as having to accept some new political strings, many other parts of the Euro-zone may well experience economic dislocation, political uncertainty and possibly social turbulence that, if unchecked, might become acute. Much will turn on whether the remarkable unity and expansion achieved by the European Community so far can be underpinned, strengthened and defended.

Another bundle of new geopolitical obstacles can be traced to the bilateral energy and financial relations of Russia and China concerning the new West-East linkage of large, brand-new long-distance oil and gas pipelines supplying Russian oil and gas to the Chinese heartland. While China can provide hard currency settlement for the Russian oil and gas supplied, there is likely to be little or no problem. Yet if Chinese infrastructure costs and global investment commitments begin to outrun the Chinese Government's export revenue and available currency reserves, there may be procrastination and confrontation ahead with China searching desperately for cheaper and more secure supply and Russia suffering from a slowdown of this hydrocarbon stream and reduced inflow of capital caused by a progressive collapse of orderly and regular settlement of these bilateral accounts.

Along Russia's southern borders, we can expect a process of tightening Russian influence and control with the present military intervention in Ukraine and the Crimea providing a severe warning and example to the other former Soviet Union states if they step too far outside the guidelines set by Moscow. This seems to suggest to me that the competing oil and gas projects of these former Soviet Union states to pipe their own oil and gas directly to China and Europe may not be as simple as they originally envisaged.

Along the North African coast, the Arab Spring of 2011 appears to have run its dismal course with planned new energy investment greatly inhibited by renewed uncertainty in Libya, Egypt and further afield as in the Sudan. This confused turmoil seems to be in danger of spreading further in Africa rather than diminishing.

For Russia, the difficulties of government in Iraq and a chaotic and complex civil war in Syria have raised high hopes in the Kremlin and excitement among the Russian populace of realising the Czarist centuries-old dream – that of eventually securing safe Russian access to a warm-water port, preferably in the Gulf – a new highway protected by Russian arms and expertise to the prime source of global energy exports. Meanwhile, Iran continues to pour arms and other support into Iraq and Syria and already exercises a significant level of control over parts of Southern Iraq.

A Fundamental Shift in Energy Import Dependency

Much will turn on the response of the United States to these new challenges from Russia and Iran. Within the energy sector, there are new realities to be faced. The continuing shift of Arabian Gulf exports of oil and gas from Western markets to China, Korea, Japan and some other South-East Asia states, already heavily dependent on hydrocarbon imports, has been accompanied by a fundamental reversal of trend in domestic hydrocarbon production in the United States. The shale surprise of the last five to ten years has transformed the United States from being a lead energy importer to become a much more significant exporter of US coal and to become the global leader in shale development and, displacing Saudi Arabia, in the production of oil and gas liquids. The new assumption that the strengthening energy independence in the United States will persist for a long time is bound to have profound impacts on US industry and on US foreign policy worldwide. In the longer-term I think (and hope) that a strengthened, less energy import dependent United States could help it to re-focus its essential leadership role in applied science and the swift commercialisation of new technology.

All in all, this litany of temporary current misery is prompting the international oil and gas industry to pull in its horns and the international investor to review much more rigorously the sharp rise in political risk. Increased insurance rates and tightening banking prudence are already bringing increased costs of these services together with greater reluctance to lend without elaborate government guarantees.

New Challenges and Opportunities

Now let us try to look on the bright side.

- *Resources of Hydrocarbon*
  All those who try to tell us, for whatever reason, that global hydrocarbon resources are being exhausted and assure us that weird and wonderful windmills, landscapes of very hot glass, megasized tide-mills and other paraphernalia will meet all our energy needs all the time within the near future are talking poppycock. Table 1 demonstrates how primary energy consumption in non-OECD countries now exceeds by a significant margin that in the OECD states. The gap will continue to widen. Yet, as demonstrated in Table 2 the bulk of proven reserves of oil, coal and gas (now including shales) remain within a quite small group of states, who control the international markets and have a strong hand in setting global energy prices. If they continue discreetly to set price parameters acceptable to the global community, this may be no bad thing. If they become divided by pandering to national interest, the chances of the global economy weathering the storm will be diminished.

  There is a strong probability that proven global reserves of oil, gas and coal will continue to rise and remain highly cost-competitive. So we may well have adequate resources to address the risk of rising global energy poverty while preventing another global conflict for resources. We do need, however, to maintain the necessary momentum of investment, security of supply, efficient global markets downstream as well as a continuing whittling down of costs through much new technology. Provided we can eliminate the environmental damage caused by this enhanced production and a more equitable sharing of global energy, we will have very little to worry about. The need to achieve a stable global understanding of these objectives and widespread co-operation, as, for example, to protect the vital energy trade routes is a prerequisite. For this we will need a new institutional framework to replace the outworn and now flawed global supervisory systems of the past seventy years.

- *Climate Change*
  On 1st November 2014, the United Nations issued its strongest warning so far of the dire consequences of continuing climate change and the need to curb the most pollutant uses of fossil energy. Rising sea-levels and urban air and water pollution were identified as major problems. The global processing of energy at

Table 1
PRIMARY ENERGY CONSUMPTION 2013
Share of global total (12730.4 million tonnes oil equivalent)

OIL	33%	ASIA PACIFIC	41%	CHINA	23%
COAL	30%	EUROPE/EURASIA	23%	USA	18%
GAS	24%	NORTH AMERICA	22%	RUSSIA	6%
HYDRO	7%	MIDDLE EAST	6%	INDIA	5%
NUCLEAR	4%	S/CENTRAL AMERICA	5%	JAPAN	4%
RENEWABLES	2%	AFRICA	3%	REST	44%

Primary Energy Consumption by non-OECD (56.5%) now exceeds OECD states (43.5%).

GLOBAL OIL CONSUMPTION 2013
Share of global total (4185.1 million tonnes)

Regions		Lead States	
ASIA PACIFIC	34%	USA	20%
NORTH AMERICA	25%	CHINA	13%
EUROPE/EURASIA	21%	RUSSIA	4%
MIDDLE EAST	9%	GERMANY	3%
S/CENTRAL AMERICA	7%	CANADA	3%
AFRICA	4%	REST	57%

Asia Pacific plus North America and Europe/Eurasia account for 80% of total Global Oil Consumption. USA leads with 20%. Russia lags with 4%.

GLOBAL GAS CONSUMPTION 2013
Share of global total (3020.4 million tonnes oil equivalent)

Regions		Lead States	
EUROPE/EURASIA	32%	USA	22%
NORTH AMERICA	28%	CHINA	5%
ASIA PACIFIC	19%	IRAN	5%
MIDDLE EAST	13%	JAPAN	4%
S/CENTRAL AMERICA	5%	CANADA	3%
AFRICA	4%	REST	61%

Europe/Eurasia plus North America and Asia Pacific account for 80% of total Global Gas Consumption. USA leads with 22%. Middle East has 13% and rising. Non-OECD has 52%, OECD 48%

GLOBAL COAL CONSUMPTION 2013
Share of global total (3826.7 million tonnes oil equivalent)

Regions		Lead States	
ASIA PACIFIC	71%	CHINA	51%
NORTH AMERICA	13%	USA	12%
EUROPE/EURASIA	13%	RUSSIA	2%
AFRICA	3%	GERMANY	2%
S/CENTRAL AMERICA	1%	REST	33%

Asia Pacific consumes 71% of total coal consumption. China consumes more than half the total Non-OECD consumes 72%; OECD 28%

Source: BP Statistical Review of World Energy, published June 2014

Table 1 (continued)

GLOBAL NUCLEAR CONSUMPTION 2013

Share of global total (563.2 million tonnes oil equivalent)

Regions		Lead States	
EUROPE/EURASIA	47%	USA	33%
NORTH AMERICA	38%	FRANCE	17%
ASIA PACIFIC	14%	RUSSIA	7%

Europe/Eurasia plus North America have 85%; USA plus France have 50%

GLOBAL HYDRO ELECTRICITY CONSUMPTION 2013

Share of global total (855.8 million tonnes oil equivalent)

Regions		Lead States	
ASIA PACIFIC	36%	CHINA	24%
EUROPE/EURASIA	24%	BRAZIL	10%
S/CENTRAL AMERICA	19%	CANADA	10%
NORTH AMERICA	18%	RUSSIA	5%

Asia Pacific plus Europe/Eurasia have 60%. China (24%) plus Brazil and Canada have 44%

RENEWABLE ENERGY (including Bio-Fuels) CONSUMPTION 2013

Share of global total (278.3 million tonnes oil equivalent)

Regions		Lead States	
EUROPE/EURASIA	41%	USA	21%
ASIA PACIFIC	28%	CHINA	15%
NORTH AMERICA	23%	GERMANY	11%

Source: BP Statistical Review of World Energy, published June 2014

locations close to the sea-shore pose particular problems for the nuclear power industry, and for the import and export terminals of oil and coal. The liquefaction and re-gasifying of natural gas have come under much closer scrutiny, while the safe storage of nuclear waste remains under review. The lesson of the past century is that the energy industries do find solutions to these problems, particularly when prompted by local disasters.

- *Alternative Energy*

    Alternative energy will have a valuable but small and costly part to play in the evolving global energy mix giving significant opportunities particularly in those states lacking domestic resources, nuclear power or hydroelectricity potential. The Achilles heel of alternative energy lies in its unpredictable intermittency, high capital and maintenance cost and dependence on rising government subsidies.

- *The Nuclear Dilemma*

    The proliferation of nuclear and chemical weapons has cast a heavy shadow over the growth of nuclear power. There have been other developments which could not have been foreseen ten years ago. The recent decisions of the Japanese government and those of Germany to scale down their nuclear generation capacity have had profound and costly impacts on the performance of their economies.

- *Extremism and Terrorism*

    We should not be too despondent about any apparently insoluble absence of geopolitical alignment or about threats from spreading extremism and terrorism. For the oil and gas industries there is now a very pressing problem. How do you protect your workers and staff in very isolated and vulnerable locations? The three global leaders, USA, China and Russia share much common ground in combating global and regional terrorism. With goodwill, solutions will be found to resolve their current conflicts of interest and, hopefully, the process of increasing consensus will be the foundation for continuing economic prosperity and greatly enhanced protection of individuals and vulnerable minorities.

- *The Role of the National Energy Companies*

    The need to protect the national interest lies behind the development of many of the leading national energy companies. Many have gone on to develop extensive interests overseas and to acquire a capability to absorb new technology and to establish new markets. Problems arise for the smaller national companies which struggle to compete against the giants in the global market for external finance, the latest equipment, skills and technology and the management of their own often highly complex development projects.

Table 2

PROVED OIL, GAS and COAL RESERVES end-2013

PROVED OIL RESERVES end-2013
Share of global total (1687.9 thousand million tonnes)

Regions		Lead States	
MIDDLE EAST	48%	VENEZUELA	18%
S/CENTRAL AMERICA	20%	SAUDI ARABIA	16%
NORTH AMERICA	14%	CANADA	10%
EUROPE/EURASIA	9%	IRAN	9%
AFRICA	8%	IRAQ	9%
ASIA PACIFIC	3%	KUWAIT	6%

Middle East has almost half the total. Venezuela plus Saudi Arabia have 34%
Oil reserves have risen steadily: increasing 62% since end-1993

PROVED GAS RESERVES end 2013
Share of global total 2013 (185.2 trillion cubic metres)

Regions		Lead States	
MIDDLE EAST	43%	IRAN	18%
EUROPE/EURASIA	31%	RUSSIA	18%
ASIA PACIFIC	8%	QATAR	13%
AFRICA	8%	USA	5%
NORTH AMERICA	6%	VENEZUELA	3%
S/CENTRAL AMERICA	4%	REST	43%

Middle East leads with 43%. Iran and Russia with Qatar account for half the total.
Total gas reserves have risen by 57% since 1993 and are rising fast with new shale and other discoveries.
Non-OECD have 90%; OECD 10%.

PROVED COAL RESERVES end 2013
Share of global total 2013 (891,531 million tonnes)

Regions		Lead States	
EUROPE/EURASIA	35%	USA	27%
ASIA PACIFIC	32%	RUSSIA	18%
NORTH AMERICA	29%	CHINA	13%
MIDDLE EAST + AFRICA	4%	INDIA	7%
S/CENTRAL AMERICA	2%	GERMANY	5%

USA (27%) together with Russia and China account for almost 60% of the total. Non-OECD states have 56.8% of the total, OECD states 43.2%. Former Soviet Union 25.6% and European Union 6.3%.

Source: BP Statistical Review of World Energy, published June 2014.

Table 3

INTERNATIONAL TRADE IN GLOBAL OIL

GLOBAL OIL EXPORTS, 2013
Million tonnes

	Crude Imports	Product Imports	Total Imports
From MIDDLE EAST	855	116	971
Former SOVIET UNION	300	145	445
WEST AFRICA	215	7	222
S/CENTRAL AMERICA	151	32	183
USA	-	151	151
NB GLOBAL TOTAL	1878	897	2775

The Middle East, mainly from the Gulf states, accounts for over one-third of the total.

GLOBAL OIL IMPORTS, 2013
Million tonnes

	Crude Imports	Product Imports	Total Imports
Into Europe	464	159	623
USA	384	99	483
CHINA	282	96	378
INDIA	191	13	204
NB GLOBAL TOTAL	1878	897	2775

Europe has the highest oil import dependency (22% of the total). USA plus China and India account for a further 38% of the total. The rest of the world has to share less than 40% of the total.

Source: BP Statistical Review of World Energy 2014, published June 2014.

- *The Role of the Multinationals*
  Generally speaking, the multinational oil and gas companies are in good shape, well-run, supported by excellent global service companies and able to perform a dynamic role in the global economy. Their accumulated skills and experience are valuable for a favourable economic outcome over the next fifty years.

- *Hybrid Development*
  The continued success of the best examples of co-operation between multinationals and national energy companies will provide an efficient model for replication widely worldwide.

Changes in Global Energy Trade and Investment

To summarise: my argument so far is that the global demand for energy looks like it will continue to accelerating faster than population growth as expectations of betterment fed by vastly improved telecommunications and enhanced personal access are experienced worldwide. We may need to plan for up to a doubling of global energy demand within fifty years, even possibly by 2050. By then we will need a whole bundle of new technology – advances in chemical energy, much more efficient energy use, nuclear fusion, breakthroughs in cheaper electricity transmission, geo-thermal, solar or whatever. Today, at least we know we have the resources to bridge the gap by expanding hydrocarbon output massively. This will require much enhanced consensus worldwide on the need for this expansion whatever increased efficiencies of energy use can meanwhile be achieved. Such an expansion requires continuity of investment and sustainability in environmental terms in a much more peaceful political environment.

Human Energy – Keep Calm but Care

Rather than go on too long about global generalities and uncertainties, I have also collected some notes and impressions based on the global, regional and national energy issues I have been involved in over the past fifty years. The UK Official Secrets Act as well as security declarations in the Bank of England, HM Treasury, Shell International, British Gas, the World Bank, World Petroleum Council and Windsor Energy inhibit me, of course, from disclosing anything that might be considered secret or confidential, including the names of those involved, but throughout all this time I kept a private notebook of those muddles and mistakes and obstacles that we encountered. Jotting them down provided a sort of therapy for the frustration, irritation and delay that they had caused. These notes also built up a useful reminder of how those obstacles were often overcome by innovative surprises, new alliances and sensitive re-thinking of the fundamental long-term interest of all the parties involved or affected. Only well-directed human energy can resolve our future trials.

After the Storm Comes the Peace

In 1954-1956 I spent my two years of National Service in the Royal Engineers where the inculcation of basic military training at Mons Officer Cadet School at Aldershot, UK proved of inestimable value later in life in the Bank of England and with Shell and elsewhere. I have long since lost my copy of the Queen's Regulations and other documentation, but fifteen of the basic points of an infantry attack were burned into my soul like a firebrand at age 18 and remain fresh in my mind to this day. They will serve here as a template for my final thoughts on the future of energy on this planet.

- *The Ultimate Objective* – What are we trying to achieve over the long-term?
- *The Immediate Objective* – What do we have to achieve now?
- *Resources* – Are they available, replenishable, cost-effective and ready to hand?
- *Intelligence* – Do we know precisely what we are up against?
- *Obstacles* – How do we eliminate the main obstacles?
- *Surprise* – How can we find answers and strike targets in new ways from new angles?
- *Superior Technology and Skills* – What are our greatest strengths?
- *Searching for Comparative Weakness* – Which gaps can we remedy?
- *Effective Communication and Co-ordination* – Can all units communicate well with an overall strategy and command centre?
- *Simple Orders* – Can all units understand their instructions and their specific role?
- *Concentration of Fire* - How can the impact of well-timed co-ordinated action be enhanced?
- *Reinforcement Options* – Where do we turn for more support?
- *Securing the Ground* – Do we have a good plan for defending the area taken?
- *Follow-up* – Unforeseen casualties? Other unforeseen consequences?
- *Contingency Planning* – What to do if resistance is stronger than expected?

I have one other point. I was not a particularly gifted soldier. Indeed I still remember the remarks expressed early each morning on the parade ground by our Regimental Sergeant Major pointing out rather loudly that my performance of the Regimental Slow March could be likened to that of a pregnant duck. He was on the right track. His job was to sharpen up our performance and in this he was remarkably successful. But from him and others much later in life I learned another lesson:

- *Do We Really Need to Resort to Military Solutions?* – What are the alternatives? We are already often well beyond the point where regional military intervention can add to global security. The need today for effective co-operation is paramount. The age of political, military and economic imperialism has largely passed. Can we secure our long-term objectives by other means: more positive, sensitive and appropriate diplomacy, a stronger case for a better sharing of resources, a building up of goodwill through better, more purpose-orientated institutions yielding strong economic and political dividends of global value?

Paul Tempest was educated on scholarships to Manchester Grammar School and Oxford where he edited *Oxford Opinion* and spent his third year in residence at the Maison Française.

At the Bank of England (1959-1983) he specialised on Western Europe, the Middle East and Global Energy with 1-2 year secondments to Switzerland (BIS), Lebanon (MECAS), Qatar and Dubai (as GM of the joint currency authority), Shell International and British Gas. He was appointed by the UK Department of Energy as the first Chairman of the British Institute of Energy Economics in 1979. Then sixth President of the IAEE in Washington DC in 1984, Head of International Energy Division in Shell (1985-91), Director-General of the World Petroleum Council (1991-99) and the Executive Director/CEO of Windsor Energy Group in 2000-09. He remains since 1985 Chairman of the Bank of England Threadneedle Club, Editor of the annual *Threadneedle* since 2002 and of *The Athenæum in Verse* since 2010 and Secretary of the Windsor Energy International Panel (since 2002). He helped M A Conant found the monthly *Geopolitics of Energy* in Washington DC (1979-93), becoming, after its transfer to the Canadian Energy Research Institute in Calgary, a member of the Editorial Board and in April 2014 one of the eight members of the Editorial Committee.

CHAPTER ONE

Plenty of Clean Energy

David Howell

If there was any doubt the plunging world crude oil price confirms it. There is a global abundance of primary energy and energy sources. There is plenty of energy. Unfortunately there are plenty of politicians as well, and plenty of political turmoil, instability and violent regional disruption across the planet.

Hence an area that should be almost free of problems – the energy supply sector - is full of problems.

The Trilemma turns into 'Trifailure'

In Europe I can report to you that these emerge in the form of an immense trilemma – not a dilemma, but a TRIlemma – a triple challenge to energy policy-makers which they are failing to meet on all three counts.

What is this 'trilemma'? It is that energy and climate policy makers have set themselves the triple goal of delivering affordable – if possible cheap – energy to consumers, that they have promised reliable supplies – no power cuts and black-outs – and that they want to see rapid decarbonisation and the replacement of fossil fuels with low carbon energy sources wherever possible.

On all three fronts they are failing spectacularly. In fact things are going the opposite way – backwards.

Affordability Abandoned

Affordability goals have been brushed aside. Indeed, energy costs are scarcely mentioned in latest EU policy documents. Yet the energy price issue is at the heart of the EU's economic future and recovery. For Poland, and not just for Poland, the huge extra costs being imposed on industry by the subsidies to expensive renewable energy are no longer bearable. The threat is to veto EU proposals for the target of

40% reduction in emissions by 2030. It would, say the Polish leaders 'destroy half of Europe's industry'.

For the domestic consumer there has been real pain. In Britain gas and electricity prices have risen, after inflation, by more than 50% in the last ten years. Meeting the European Union targets for reducing carbon emission – 80% by 2050 – would involve equally large future increases to raise the funds to pay for the gigantic subsidies to renewable energy – notably wind – required.

The EU target would mean covering an impossibly large area of Europe with turbines at a cost of 3.2 trillion Euros – most of it to be squeezed from consumers. And all this while the actual cost of primary energy supplies – gas, oil and coal – are actually falling!

But Emissions are Rising

All this would be tolerable if these policies were the essential way to guarantee reliable electricity supplies, to cut the growth of carbon emissions and perform a worthwhile role in combatting climate change globally.

But they are doing no such thing.

As old coal-fired stations in Europe are closed they are being replaced not by reliable generating sources – such as gas turbines, or new nuclear stations, but by intermittent sources such as wind, which themselves require new gas fired plant to back them up when the wind does not blow, or blows too hard.

But the investment in new gas capacity is not going ahead, because the Government–imposed penalties on gas burning make it unprofitable. In Britain some quite new gas turbines are being shut down.

And meanwhile new nuclear stations are far too expensive. In Germany they are being closed down altogether. In Britain a new station, Hinckley Point C, has been cajoled into being by hideously high guaranteed price promises for years to come, penalising future generations – although it will anyway take a decade to build.

Meanwhile the spare generating capacity to meet crises or times of extra heavy power demand has dwindled to a wafer-thin margin, and may well lead to black-outs.

The final irony is that in an effort to counteract this chaos new coal stations are being built in Europe and much more cheap coal being imported – from Russia, America and elsewhere.

The net effect of all these policy blunders is that carbon emissions are rising, not falling - in Germany dramatically so. Even if carbon emissions from production and electric power have fallen with recession in Europe, carbon consumption per head has soared as carbon-intensive imports pour into European markets.

There is not the slightest chance that carbon reduction targets in Europe will be achieved. So while the threat to our global environment is not being met, the costs of these ineffective policies are rising exponentially.

Effective Clean Energy Policies Rejected

Common sense tells us how to reverse these trends and help rather than damage our environment. In theory it should be easy. Burning gas emits at least 40% less carbon than oil or coal, as the American example of switching from coal to gas demonstrates. It has been estimated by BP that a switch of one percent of global power generation from coal to gas, would produce carbon emission savings the equivalent of increasing renewables by 11%.

And if only nuclear power construction costs could be reduced that would really set us on the path to curbing CO^2 growth.

But in practice energy policy in Europe is taking us directly the other way.

Gas is being taxed and its global trade impeded. New gas developments –e.g. fracking – are being resisted or forbidden. Nuclear power progress is being stymied by politics. Renewables, instead of benefitting from new technology, are sucking up subsidies and enriching the powerful at the expense of the weak. Oil is full of dangers from the Middle East, and from refinery and transport challenges. Coal is getting a free rein and is expanding its grip on world energy production.

Those of us who are deeply concerned about potential resumption of global warming – after the present pause of the past eighteen years – have a right to be furious at these appalling policy failures. The entire process has rightly been called by some 'insane'.

Reversal: Some Practical Solutions Now

But what are the practical solutions? How do we counter massive incompetence and misunderstanding, starting from here?
1. The whole attitude to gas production, transmission and use has to be transformed, and gas seen not as an enemy of a greener world, but as its most powerful friend – the best pathway to the future.
2. Huge efforts MUST be made to design and build cheaper and safer nuclear power plants, maybe building on a much smaller scale. No more Hinckley Cs!

3. Coal-burning can be met half-way not by banning it but by super-efficient new methods, super-critical boiler technology, more efficient transmission and a host of other improvements.
4. Resources now going to subsidise inefficient and costly renewables, such as offshore wind, should now be diverted to all-out efforts to make greener energy CHEAPER, not far more expensive. It is the sheer forces of ingenuity and competition that must be allowed to do the job. Solar power is already benefitting – slowly. Wind power must respond in the same way.
5. Technology must be allowed to deliver to the producer, the transmitter and the end consumer of fuel and power the enormous efficiency gains that are just around the corner. Final demand can be held flat even with a growing world population, and even with the full development needs of the awakening giants like China and India being recognised and respected.

The Lessons that Must Now be Learned

The lessons of the present disasters and backward steps are;
1. That bracketing ALL fossil fuels together as anti-environmental undermines far the best environmental and green way forward. It causes great pain and suffering to the world's poorest and slows growth.
2. It has inevitably produced a major and angry reaction from consumers the world over, and especially throughout Europe. Sensible and constructive green policies have been destroyed by blind zealotry.
3. If policy-makers and politicians will disengage and stop distorting markets and investment, new technology and competition, and the world-wide urge to have cheaper, cleaner and green power, now almost universal, will deliver strong results and our planet will survive and prosper.

At Last

There are, to repeat, plentiful supplies of all kinds of cleaner, greener energy available to all the world's peoples, rich and poor. It is the present blind and perverse policies of too many politicians, and too many misguided lobbies, which are stopping them having it. Our world is indeed being endangered, and much harm being done to our environment and to future generations, through the energy and failed climate policies that have been pursued – both in Britain, in most of Europe and in some other nations as well, although thankfully not all.

At last some people are beginning to speak up. At last what some have been warning about for a decade past is beginning to prompt changed thoughts and a better new direction – both for the planet and all its peoples.

Text of speech by Lord Howell of Guildford, Chairman of the Windsor Energy Group, to the WEG Tokyo Roundtable, Bloomberg Office, Tokyo, Thursday 23 October 2014.

Lord Howell of Guildford PC

David Howell is a former Secretary-of-State for Energy (i.e., the UK Energy Minister, 1979–81), Secretary-of-State for Transport, 1981–83) and previously the Minister of State in the Northern Ireland Office (1972-74). More recently, he has been until mid-2013 Minister for the Commonwealth in the Foreign and Commonwealth Office and simultaneously Minister for International Energy Security. He was educated at Eton and King's College, Cambridge, UK, winning a first class BA degree with his attention focussed particularly on politics, economics and history. While Minister of Energy in 1979, he helped found the British Institute of Energy Economics and has just completed the 9-year (maximum) term as President (2004–2013). Since 2004 he has also been Chairman of the Windsor Energy Group.

David Howell's books include: *Blind Victory* (1986); *The Edge of Now* (2000); *Out of the Energy Labyrinth* (with co-author Carole Nakhle, 2007, I B Tauris); *Old Links and New Ties* (with co-author Carole Nakhle, 2013, I B Tauris) .

CHAPTER TWO

Energy Imbroglio

David Howell

(OED. Imbroglio: a state of confused entanglement: a complicated or difficult situation: a serious misunderstanding)

For politicians and the policy-making world, energy issues have a particular characteristic. They lie quiescent for long periods while society enjoys, indeed takes for granted, plentiful and uninterrupted supplies of fuel and power at reasonable cost. Then suddenly, like a sleeping snake uncoiling, they leap up and grab government by the throat, disrupting everyday life and economic activity, generating unforeseen collateral damage, and threatening the very survival of governments. Such a time has arrived recently for a number of governments, especially in Europe and especially in Britain.

Energy Prospects are Changing Swiftly

Today, energy fortunes are changing all across the planet, not least the fortunes of numerous Commonwealth countries in Africa and Asia as well as the fortunes of Britain itself. What is the biggest single cause of this change? It is the extraordinary and largely unpredicted shale oil and gas revolution and the associated improved technologies for recovering oil and gas economically which underlie it. Unbelievable five years ago, the USA is now producing more liquid petroleum than any other country in the world, an increase of over 50% over the last three years while shale gas is displacing coal throughout the US economy. Saudi Arabia which has held the No.1 position for over 20 years is now urged into a policy of cutting oil production to prop up the global oil price. In political and economic terms, higher output in the USA has reduced the ability of OPEC led by Saudi Arabia to control global energy pricing while at the same time downgrading somewhat the interest of the USA in protecting the energy supply security of the rest of the world.

The losers in this new power game will be those countries who burden themselves with expensive energy, with low investment in new energy and electricity supply facilities, and with a hesitant approach to new resource development.

Britain has half tumbled into the second category, struggling to modernise the nuclear sector, which ought to have been transformed thirty years ago, and handicapping itself with expensive power, ensuring low investment in new energy facilities, and offering only a hesitant welcome to resource development. All this adds a heavy burden to the British economy, weakens its capacity to participate in the global energy revolution, and slows down both economic and social progress.

In the wider world energy scene, accepted wisdom has been overtaken. Middle East oil and gas dominance, OPEC power, Russian Gazprom gas monopoly, peak oil and gas – all the foundations of twentieth century concern about energy security – are beginning to crumble and collapse.

This may sound as if it belongs more in the hard real world of power and resources than in the digital age. But in fact it is microchip technology and information expansion which has opened out the new resource pattern, while the network world is more heavily dependent than ever on totally reliable and affordable electricity and energy supplies. Indeed, it is cheap and plentiful power supplies which hold the key to the defeat of world poverty as well as to the return of prosperity to the already industrialised world.

The global transformation in the pattern of energy resources, driven by the shale oil and gas revolution, is changing the face and future of numerous countries, previously believed to be, and feeling themselves to be, well out in the cold and irretrievably dependent on others for their daily energy supplies. African nations are especially well-placed in this scene.

An Opportunity for the UK

All this ought to be of major advantage to the UK in world markets. In Sub-Saharan Africa alone there are more than half a dozen Commonwealth member states pondering how to exploit large new fossil fuel resources commercially. British firms are extraordinarily adept at helping development in the kind of offshore conditions these countries face (other examples include Kenya, Tanzania, Mozambique, and South Africa; and on the Atlantic side, Sierra Leone, the Nigerian giant, and Ghana). The smaller Commonwealth states, many of them with highly constrained economies, face horrendously high prices for imported diesel and long to find ways to move to both cheaper and cleaner energy sources. British ingenuity and experience, built up on both North Sea and world-wide experience, ought to be well qualified to help.

In addition, Britain itself at home is, or ought to be, superbly placed and highly attractive to new overseas investors in manufacturing electricity generating plants and equipment, the design of more advanced transmission systems, and more efficient electricity and energy usage. Out of the renewed interest in North Sea oil and gas and onshore shale oil and gas, there are likely to be opportunities for a revived supply industry serving the world market and for the UK to market its expertise in new refinery and petrochemical products in close co-operation with the leading international exploration, refining, and operating and servicing companies.

Vast Resources of UK Coal and Plentiful Gas, Shale and Oil

Britain holds vast resources of coal and still plentiful North Sea gas and oil – its neighbours are clamouring for more British piped gas – especially Norway but also Russia via its proposed branch line from Nordstream to East Anglia. Britain also holds a very large on-shore shale gas potential. Suppliers round the world are eager to ship more frozen gas (LNG), and the UK has excellent and growing facilities to receive LNG and transmit it into the high quality gas grid. There is plenty of wind and tide potential in the UK, long and deep civil nuclear experience (despite the setbacks of the last century), top quality skills, and innovative power both in conventional oil and gas development, production, and transmission and in green and energy efficient technologies.

This ought to be the ideal recipe for reliable, low-cost, sustainable energy supplies to power the British economy for ages to come, not to mention well-heated and comfortable homes for the British population indefinitely into the future at prices they can afford with ease. Energy policy should be pushing Britain forward, not holding it back.

The UK pricing nonsense

Something is badly wrong. Instead of plentiful, cheap, and reliable power supplies, we have the opposite – an energy imbroglio with uncertainty. Today we have eye-watering price increases, and real fear of power failures stalking the scene. British energy prices are said to be some of the highest in Europe and the world and are set to rise higher still.[1] Britain's energy policy ought to be the least controversial and smoothest running part of government. Instead it is locked into out-of-date commitments and strategies, broadly labelled 'The Green Transition', and largely dictated and corralled by equally dated EU energy policy requirements. The result is delusion on a grand scale, and chaos.

This is not just bar room grumbling at ever higher energy bills. It is an unavoidable conclusion I have reached after serving for two-and-a-half years as international energy security minister, serving the same length of time as Secretary of State for Energy in Margaret Thatcher's time, having written books and countless articles on energy issues, and having followed every twist and turn of energy issues in many countries over a period of thirty years.[2]

To repeat, we in the British Isles are in energy chaos. None of our objectives will be reached. All are severely threatened.

The UK Shortfall in New Power Generation was Easily Avoidable

Investment in new power generation at the required level is not occurring; power shortages, interruptions, and black-outs are in prospect; carbon reduction targets will not be reached; energy costs are internationally uncompetitive; energy prices are stupidly high, and fuel poverty is at record levels; the attempt to reincarnate the nuclear power programme is once again faltering; the environment is being desecrated (a true irony when the main Green objective is supposed to be to protect our environment); more coal is being burnt than ever (another irony and direct result of Green policies); participation in the shale gas and oil revolution is hesitant; worldwide British involvement in the effects of this revolution, and in its transforming impact on the whole of global energy ought to be much greater, what with British North Sea experience and two of the biggest energy companies in the world on our shores.

Despite being highly favourably placed to enjoy secure and cheap energy supplies for years to come, our policy has set Britain in the opposite direction, towards insecurity, higher and higher costs, greater pollution, and massive environmental damage – quite an achievement.

British energy policy-makers and commentators speak of an energy 'trilemma'. The

---

1   The Market Oracle, 17th May 2013.
2   I have also been President of the British Institute of Energy Economics for nine years and am President of the Energy Industries Council.

**Photographs taken in Windsor Castle during the
Windsor Energy Group Consultations 28 February to 2 March 2014**

HE Khaled Al-Duwaisan
Ambassador of Kuwait and Dean of the London Diplomatic Corps

Lord (David) Howell of Guildford PC (left) and HE Kamalesh Sharma, Secretary-General of the Commonwealth and guest speaker at the 2014 Ambassadors' Dinner.

Left:
Lord (Ron) Oxburgh of Liverpool

Below:
Lord Howell of Guildford PC

Above and right:
The Windsor Energy Group in session in the Vicars' Hall

Below:
Ian Walker, Executive Director of the Windsor Energy Group

Lady (Barbara) Judge, Chair Emeritus of the UK Atomic Energy Authority

The Windsor Energy Group leaving Vicars' Hall for lunch in St George's House

Above: **A briefing in the Dungeon**

Below left: **Stephen Nash** cmg, WEG Adviser on the Former Soviet Union

Below right: **Paul Tempest**, Secretary of the International Panel

need, they say, is to reconcile three key objectives in this field – affordability, reliability, and security of environmentally acceptable supply (namely decarbonisation targets).

Regrettably, the record is one of failure on all three fronts. High and ever-rising prices are causing dismay amongst both domestic and industrial consumers; power shortages and possible cuts are being widely forecast; and green, or low carbon, objectives are not being genuinely met.

Two Energy Revolutions

The background to this unpromising scene has been shaped by two energy revolutions. The first, familiar to almost every policy-maker on the planet, is the push towards low carbon technologies, an attempt to move away from fossil fuels to new and renewable energy sources – thereby somehow checking feared global warming. The second, much less familiar to policy-makers and politicians, is the shale gas and shale oil revolution.

The second upheaval is having far greater impact on all our lives than the first, although the two interact. The shale gas phenomenon opens the gate to almost unlimited supplies of hydrocarbons at relatively modest cost. It thereby greatly increases the subsidies, taxes, and higher charges necessary to finance and install much more expensive renewables, such as wind power, solar power, and nuclear power – the latter not counted as renewable by the true green hot gospellers but in fact offering power with far less carbon and on a far greater scale than any other source.

The Global Impact of Shale

The discovery of vast new shale gas deposits all round the world, even if so far only developed and extracted mainly in the US, has made the scares about peak oil and gas obsolete. The doomsters have fallen silent about the world running out of gas and oil. This comes at the same time when deep, pre-salt oil has been found in prodigious quantities off the shores of Brazil, when in Canada major new oil discoveries are being registered, over and above the rapidly growing oil sands output, when Venezuela has discovered much more oil, and when possibilities for extracting gas and oil from the Arctic region at commercial rates are growing rapidly. In the Middle East, a stabilised Iraq and less hostile Iran could rapidly add another 15 mbdoe to global energy supply

All this has also put a question mark over previous energy policy assumptions that wholesale oil and gas prices are bound to go on rising. Scores more countries are set to become gas and oil producers, and exporters, while America's imports are declining at the same time as its production is soaring. This entirely new energy situation has produced conflicting responses from national governments. There is a tug of war in policy-making between the network world and energy independence and security. The transformed global energy system, with its maze of pipelines, transmission systems, and interconnectors, clearly offers dazzling network and market advantages in terms of commercial gain and supply diversity. Any national energy planner anywhere can see that.

But it also offers dangers. At the other end of the connection, something might happen. At the other end of the contract pipeline or supply chain, there can be overthrown governments, terrorist attacks, piracy, disasters – man-made or otherwise. The instinct to keep it all at home, to keep as many energy supply sources on safe sovereign soil, becomes ever stronger.

Such a view has entirely taken over American energy policy. Energy independence has become the national mantra, the implausible dream. Articulated by successive Presidents from Jimmy Carter onwards, now, through no hand of Government, the dream is seemingly about to become reality. Salvation comes through fracking,[3] by access to gas and oil deposits at commercially feasible costs, and on an unprecedented and undreamed of scale.

The New Search for Energy Independence

Expanded oil and gas production on the phenomenal American scale may not be available in the rest of the world, but the instincts to search for independence, and the sense of safety and security it brings, are there in many countries. China longs for reduced reliance on foreigners, even while hoovering up hydrocarbon concessions round the world. European states yearn to be out from under Gazprom (in effect Russian Government) dependency. France long ago made the mighty decision to build its way out of Arab oil reliance with fifty-eight new nuclear reactor plants.

Almost all other existing or potential major energy producers are thinking in terms of self-sufficiency as the first priority, with exports coming a hopeful second.

Actually, the sense of security from self-sufficiency can be false. Britain found this out through bitter experience in the 1960s and 1970s when it relied overwhelmingly

---

3 A truly ugly word, short of course for hydraulic fracturing of deep-lying shale rock from which gas is released in prodigious quantities by water pressure, combined with sand and chemicals.

for electricity generation on domestic coal supplies. The miners struck and Britain was paralysed. 'Never again' was the lesson.

How UK Thinking May Need to Change

But now the thinking may need to change once more. With North Sea oil and gas production lower (although not falling half as fast as many experts predicted), and with imports rising, the dangers of too much import dependence begin to be appreciated again. Imported frozen gas (LNG) now meets 38% of daily UK requirements – the bulk of it for gas turbines to produce electricity (roughly 40-45% most days). Eighty percent of that comes from Qatar via a continuous sea chain of LNG (Liquid Natural Gas) tankers to the UK and could be a case of too many eggs in one basket. It gives renewed significance to the advantages of domestic shale gas recovery onshore in the UK, as well as to further North Sea incentives.

How can Britain sort out its energy future as it struggles to find a way through all these dilemmas, or in this case the so-called trilemma of reconciling cost and security of supply with green and low carbon objectives? A confident nation, on the forward foot internationally, needs sound energy and power. Despite the present muddle, there is a pathway out to a much safer, cheaper, and altogether more reliable future.

Out of the Imbroglio

The gateway to a better route surely comes through acceptance of a new and different approach to the green economy goal. The real green transition will come not through higher energy prices but through lower ones. Once cleaner power sources become cheaper than coal, oil, or gas, the market will work and the consumer switch to low carbon energy sources will begin on a massive scale, but not before.

The driver for lower costs is, of course, technical innovation. It is new, cleverer and cheaper ways of harnessing wind, solar, wave, and nuclear energy and bringing down the costs of providing power from these sources which will motivate change. Public resources should therefore be heavily focussed on promoting research and innovation and cost-saving technical advances in all the renewable areas, rather than on subsidising already installed high-cost renewables, such as wind farms. The key is new technology. Public support ought to focus on research and development on every part of the power supply chain from generation, to transmission, to distribution, and to efficiency in consumption.[4] Make all these things cheaper, and they will be adopted. Make and deliver more electricity out of a tonne of coal, a barrel of oil, a therm of gas, make better transmission lines which lose less power along the way, and the investment will be forthcoming. Make energy saving equipment in the factory or office, and energy saving items in the home, cheaper and more efficient, and they will be installed and used.

Not Much Hope at Present

Exactly the opposite approach now prevails in British energy policy. It is to make energy supplies more expensive, based on the theory that high energy costs will lead to more energy saving expenditures and one day lower bills. It is to support and subsidise not research and innovation but actual operation of lower efficiency and very costly renewable energy installations, especially wind farms. Subsidising high cost wind farm operations is, of course, a direct disincentive to look for cheaper methods and better technologies. If the returns are now flowing in, what is the point of shifting to new machinery? If wind farms can be built and operated in ways which pull in large subsidies, whether paid for by the taxpayer or the already burdened consumer, where is the case for tiresome efforts to find new technologies and installing new systems?

But if high subsidies to inherently non-commercial renewable energy systems discourage innovation they also have two other killer features. The first is that subsidising renewable energy undermines investment in new fossil fuel power plants, however efficient, and however effective in reducing carbon emissions, however necessary in replacing old and dirtier generating equipment and power stations. Why should investors risk their funds for projects which are not only going to be up against unfair and subsidised competition, but may actually carry extra handicaps in the form of carbon taxes, further costly design requirements, and other burdens?

They will not do it. The new investment in gas turbines will not take place. At the time of writing, only one gas-fired plant is under construction out of at least thirty promised and needed to replace old coal burning stations. The old plant will have to be repaired and its life stretched. Coal-fired plants will be kept burning away, and new ones may even be built, especially if coal supplies are plentiful and cheap and especially if even cheaper coal is on offer from the United States, where the switch to cheap gas on

---

4 Cost estimates for wind electricity at the time of writing are 100 pence per kilowatt hour average for electricity onshore wind pylons, and 190 pence from offshore pylons. The current cost from conventional plants is 50 pence. Families and firms pay the difference.

a vast scale has left coal suppliers eager to find new markets.

Thus, perversity of perversities, heavily subsidised renewables deter new gas-fired turbines however much carbon they save, leaving more coal-burning to fill the gap.

Hardest Hit are Millions of the Poorest Families

But if that is not bad enough – and of course dangerous enough, since it imperils future energy security, as well as climate security – an even bigger negative factor is at work. High 'green' subsidies (in fact barely green at all) have to be paid for. Consumers and taxpayers have to foot the bill. In an era when taxes are already high, when living standards are being squeezed and when energy costs are already far above historical levels anyway, policies to raise them further are guaranteed to produce very strong reaction and resistance. Hardest hit are millions of the poorest families.[5] Ever bigger sums have to be carved out of weekly household budgets to pay the subsidies which wind farm operators enjoy. The transfer is from the poor to the rich on a substantial scale. It is an un-saleable political message, running counter to the best ideals in all the political parties. The green cause, at first so broadly supported and popular, has become discredited and unpopular. Incompetent handling and messaging is betraying the good green case.

Thus the resources which should be going into inventing new technologies for processing, transporting, and consuming power in the electric age, are being dissipated in the most wasteful and counterproductive ways. A Britain that ought to be basking in plentiful, secure, and affordable energy supplies, and pushing forward inventively towards a greener power supply pattern and a modernised energy infrastructure, has saddled itself instead with a risky, hyper-expensive, and largely un-modernised energy system.

The Green Transition is Bound to Collapse

The Green Transition was originally a scenario drawn up in 2009 by the UK's gas and electricity regulator, Ofgem. A price was put on it of £240 billion. One estimate is that the effect on average household energy bills will be to raise them from 2012s £1243 to 2020s £4733 – in real terms.[6] In practice, the Green Transition will prove impossible to deliver. Consumers are not going to pay these sums and will vote against the Government that

---

5   The most recent official estimate at the time of writing is that seven million UK families face fuel poverty, and over half of all households owe money to their energy suppliers.

6   Figures from the Price Comparison website Uswitch.com.

tries to impose them. The investing companies, the Big Six and the National Grid, will not be able to afford the investment involved. The problems of balancing electricity supply with the enormous wind power element involved (some 30% of supply capacity) will be unmanageable. A massive countryside reaction against the cat's cradle of new grid pylons, wind pylons, switching stations, and supporting road infrastructure, led by environmentalists from both left and right politically, will make progress impossible. Above all, the widening availability of gas, driven by the shale phenomenon, will make unfinanceable the very high cost of renewable supplies and technology.

This gaping, self-inflicted wound weakens the British economy, weakens its competitiveness, and weakens its capacity to join in the energy revolution round the world in which numerous countries are beginning to participate – many of them members of the Commonwealth. A more negative and myopic set of policies could scarcely be devised by Britain's worst enemies. They should now be reversed in favour of cheaper power, lower energy bills, and the maximum support for new energy technologies at every level.

New Nuclear Investment will be Delayed

A little further ahead lies the need for Britain to renew its outworn nuclear power fleet of generating stations. But the timing of new nuclear investment needs to be carefully dovetailed with the now prolonged age of gas which seems likely to fill at least the next decade or more. With the major expansion of gas availability through shale gas, the 'stepping stone' nature of the gas era becomes greatly extended as part of the pathway to low carbon. The tipping point will be the moment – not easy to define – when natural gas costs in Europe look set to rise sharply and new nuclear power costs begin to fall with the deployment of new technology. At this point, the heavy subsidy required for nuclear build (via either taxation or extra consumer burdens) will begin to ease.

The deal agreed upon between EDF (Areva) and the British Government to build two new reactors of 1,300 megawatts each at Hinkley Point, and possibly two more at Sizewell in Suffolk, does not seem to fit into this necessary sequencing. Unless and until the shale gas revolution collapses – which appears extremely unlikely for decades ahead – and the natural gas price then soars in all regions, the subsidy element for new nuclear, expressed through agreeing a strike price for the electricity generated from the new plant for thirty-five years ahead at a level roughly twice the present average generating cost (£92.50 per megawatt hour as opposed to a current £50 per megawatt hour) remains exorbitant.

By implication it appears that those who have struck the Hinkley nuclear deal want to by-pass the gas age completely, keep gas prices high, discourage gas turbine building, and leap frog prematurely into the first available nuclear deal to hand. In doing so they are buying for Britain what is basically an outdated nuclear technology (pressurised water) with a number of modifications (to the so-called EPR – European Pressurised Water Reactor) which have yet to show results or deliver a successful, on-time or on-budget completion. And it may well be that they are buying too soon. Other, cheaper and more reliable technologies, such as the Advanced Boiling Water Reactor (already in a number of places up and running reliably) are coming along. They will take longer to licence but a wait might be prudent anyway.

Such is the price, and behaviour pattern, of zealous policy-makers who, having opposed and delayed new nuclear power stations for too long, suddenly realise that low carbon objectives cannot possibly be replaced without nuclear power; they have rushed with the zealotry of converts to the first available nuclear project on offer – a European one with Chinese financial support (which may lead to direct managerial involvement later).

Even Greater Confusion in Europe

The wider European energy scene provides the context for all that is happening, and going wrong, on the domestic British energy front. The British imbroglio is part and parcel of an even greater confusion at the European level. It should not be so, but it is.

Huge divergences have been opening up between European official aims for energy and climate security, American and wider world experience; as well as huge differences between policy aspirations and intentions and what is actually happening.

Official EU energy and climate policy aims are:

- A 20% reduction by 2020 in EU greenhouse gas emissions from 1990 levels;
- Raising the share of EU energy consumption produced from renewable resources to 20%;
- A 20% improvement in the EU's energy efficiency.

The targets were set by EU leaders in March 2007, when they committed Europe to become a highly energy-efficient, low carbon economy, and were enacted through the climate and energy package in 2009. The EU is also offering to increase its emissions reduction to 30% by 2020 if other major economies in the developed and developing worlds commit to undertake their fair share of a global emissions reduction effort.

The 20-20-20 targets represent what is claimed to be an integrated approach to climate and energy policy that aims to combat climate change, increase the EU's energy security, and strengthen its competitiveness. They are also headline targets of the Europe 2020 strategy for smart, sustainable, and inclusive growth. This is meant to reflect the recognition, or hope, that tackling the climate and energy challenge will contribute to the creation of jobs, the generation of 'green' growth, and a strengthening of Europe's competitiveness.

The measures and legislation enacted to 'deliver' these targets will achieve none of their objectives. They are based on delusion. Greenhouse gases will not be curbed globally; in net terms, jobs are being lost on a major scale – not increased – as European industrial energy costs soar and investment goes elsewhere; renewable energy targets will not be met. Indeed, the 'dirtiest' of all fossil fuels, coal, is gaining a dominant role in European power generation.

EU Energy Policy is Dubious

On paper the low carbon objective may be met but this is a statistical twist. Continued recession, with zero EU growth, temporarily holds down the official figure but carbon comes pouring in with imports. Suppliers to European markets switch their sources to China and other exporters where manufacturing carries on without too much concern for emissions restraint and without penalties. This is the phenomenon of so-called carbon leakage and it means, of course, that the total official figure of carbon emitted to meet European consumer needs is a bit of a cheat.

Meanwhile, the large subsidies required to make renewable energy systems viable have to be borne by both homes and industries, making European manufacturing increasingly uncompetitive. Little notice gets taken of the warnings from one industrial leader after another that while the US is 'running away' with the shale revolution, European manufacturers are facing 'crippling energy costs' with the trade gap between the US and Europe rising to its highest level in twenty years. The gap is forecast to widen further in the years ahead.[7]

The EU carbon trading scheme adds to the burdens without making any discernible

---

7   See for example, the comments of Marcus Beyrer, head of Business Europe, speaking of the grim implications of Europe's high cost energy policies for the chemical industry. His voice is one of many. Senior Shell executive Andy Brown spoke of 'a ridiculous situation' where 'cash-strapped Europe is putting a lot of money into renewables ... meanwhile allowing the power generators to take much more coal and back out gas'. (*Daily Telegraph* April 2013).

contribution to reduced emissions. The so-called Emissions Trading Mechanism (ETM) is in practice a flop. So many permits have been issued to industry by nervous authorities that the price of emitting carbon has fallen to less than £4 a tonne, a tiny deterrent to carbon-intensive operations. The ETM is another good example of the clash between economic theory and practical reality.

On paper, the idea of issuing permits to emit CO^2 and then allowing those who do not use them up to sell to other emitters ought to work smoothly. Unfortunately, it overlooks politics and the human factor. Industries and big emitters have lobbies. Lobbies bring pressure to bear on policy-makers and Ministers. Ministers want to keep above the fray and retain elector confidence. To do that they issue more permits to the industries under pressure. The price of permits falls and the disincentives to carbon emissions evaporate. Theory is trumped by human behaviour.

A Stupendous, Costly and Hurtful Error

All this is turning out to be a stupendous error, and costly and hurtful error at that. Had Barbara Tuchman lived on into the present age, this could well have been one of the milestones in her onward march of establishment folly. At root, Europe's well-intentioned policy-makers have been fed with bad guidance, leading them to believe that greenhouse gases can be controlled, and global warming curbed, relatively cheaply, straightforwardly, and swiftly. It turns out that the costs of transforming energy systems to more sustainable patterns are proving far higher than predicted by experts and the gains far more ambiguous and indefinite.

A major culprit here has been the widely acclaimed but deeply misleading Stern Review, published in October 2006.[8] This argued that serious measures to avert global warming could be put in place relatively inexpensively if early action was taken. But the costs which consumers have been asked to bear have already proved much higher, and the persuasive powers of the message much weaker than the optimists or the supposedly expert analysts hoped for.

As I argued in a book co-authored with Dr Carole Nakhle in 2007,[9] the appeal to consumers to pay painful extra costs to save the planet at some distant future date would not be sufficient. The message was wrong. A far more compelling theme would have been that it was future energy security that necessitated a shift to low carbon

---

8 The Stern Review. Report by Sir Nicholas Stern (now Lord Stern) *The Economics of Climate Change.* October 2006.

9 Out of the Energy Labyrinth, I B Tauris 2007.

power and that green technologies (including nuclear power) could in due course produce cheaper instead of painfully more expensive energy supplies, as well as safer and more reliable power sources. The Al Gore appeal – that saving the planet required sacrifice now, and that the science of imminent doom was settled beyond dispute, was never going to carry enough people with it. Vague, weak, and implausible messages were always going to produce bad results, and this has proved to be the case. In Britain intense hostility has now built up against the green cause.

A Government in Britain which wanted to be 'the greenest government ever' has found itself on the defensive and on the retreat over its energy pricing policies. Two further problems are undermining the green case.

The EU has had No Effect on China, USA and Russia

First, it is evident to the most casual observer that Europe's 'example' to the world's biggest carbon emitters – notably China, USA, and Russia – is having no effect whatsoever. Despite strong concern within the Chinese hierarchy about pollution, especially sulphur pollution from coal burning, CO^2 emissions in that nation continue to soar, adding more each year than Britain's total annual emissions. Ironically, America is achieving big reductions in carbon emissions but not through taxes and high cost energy, not through following the European example, and not through any kind of commitment to the protocols originally agreed at Kyoto in 2003.

Instead the drivers have been technology, innovation, and cheap power. China's green achievements, such as they are, and its commitment to renewable energy sources, mainly wind power, are being driven almost entirely by the wish for greater energy security and the desire to be independent of outside supplies. If any example is being followed in Beijing, it is more the American than the European one. If Europe's example is having no influence, why, it is asked, do the extra burdens have to be borne? What is the purpose? Where are the results? Why does so much diplomatic effort need to be expended seeking the holy grail of a global commitment to legally binding carbon emissions targets when no such goal is remotely attainable? Already, the IPCC is beginning to modify its position in light of the recent changes in the global energy market and the slow progress achieved so far.

As each international gathering takes place to monitor world progress in the battle against destructive climate change, these are the questions that get asked but receive no answers. The battle is being lost through political incompetence and poor messaging, and everyone knows it.

The Voice of the People Will Prevail

People will make sacrifices and accept extra burdens on their budgets and family lives if they are persuaded that the benefits are real. But in this respect the scientific community, and its supporting lobbies, have let the green cause down badly. This author has no sympathy with those preaching the outright denial of concerns about the climate. He believes that terrible climate violence could be coming, that amongst many causes of these man-made greenhouse gases could be one, and that preparations and steps are possible to mitigate, adjust to and, just possibly, delay the threat.

But the spurious precision given to the prospects, and the dictatorial tone in which forecasts are handed down, have all added to the backlash. Green extremism, and the over-hasty rush to decarbonise, have together all but destroyed the green case. Underhanded methods by organisations such as Greenpeace, of which this author has personal experience, and intolerant zealotry in the face of scientific hesitations, have all further compounded the doubts about sustainable energy measures and whether the costs are worthwhile.

The Catastrophic Policies of the EU must be Challenged

Britain should be campaigning vigorously to change the direction of the EU Commission's ineffective and catastrophic policies. The focus of European energy policy needs to be on energy market liberalisation and on a much expanded infrastructure of gas and electricity pipelines and connectors to ensure reliability and avoid power breakdowns. This approach should be folded into the broader case for EU reforms for which the British Prime Minister has been pressing and for which millions of European citizens now long.

The twin hearts of the problem are two EU directives, both now badly out of date. One, the EU Large Combustion Plants Directive, requires the rapid closure of many older power stations, regardless of the risks to supply security. The other is the EU Renewables directive compelling Britain to generate at least 15% of its total energy from renewables (defined not to include nuclear power) – a requirement which effectively means that the electricity generating sector will have to find 30% from renewable sources. Hence the enormous drive to promote and subsidise wind farms.

It cannot be done. It is essential that the straightjacket on Britain is released and the EU directive renegotiated. For it is this, above all, and more than any other factor, which is propelling Britain away from sound and sustainable energy and towards a hobbled, constricted, and – literally – darker future. Those who entrusted their political leaders in Europe with the task of supervising a great transformation to an age of cleaner, safer, greener, and more affordable energy have been betrayed and are entitled to be angry. A clear-thinking Britain should be angry, too. Energy-related issues bring down Ministers and Governments, and have done so in several countries, including Britain, in living memory. Instead of 'stumbling towards crisis', in the words of Dieter Helm, Oxford Professor of Energy, a confident British nation should be leading Europe away from crisis and towards green policies which are viable, affordable, and assist economic recovery. And based on firm ground at home it should also build its muscle as a major supplying power of energy equipment, services and skills, using the Commonwealth network as one of its most valuable outlets. And it should start now.[10]

A Fundamental National Objective

High cost energy, mishandled energy transition, and misguided EU policies are holding Britain back and preventing it from making full use of its immense network advantages. They tie a boulder to the foot of the runner in the global race. They damage the green cause, weaken industrial success and undermine competitiveness. In the new phase of Britain's journey into the network age, they must be taken off the train and left behind.

This chapter draws on views expressed in Lord Howell's two latest books (*Out of the Energy Labyrinth* and *Old Links and New Ties*) and on recent articles published in *Geopolitics of Energy*, *Petroleum Review* and *IAEE Energy Forum*.

---

10   See Professor Dieter Helm in the magazine *Prospect*, April 2013. See also his intensely illuminating work 'The Carbon Crunch', Yale University Press, 2012.

CHAPTER THREE

US Energy Policy

Dr Herman Franssen

President Obama's Energy Policy

Candidate Obama was faced with major energy challenges in 2008 ranging from the reality that replacing fossil fuels with renewable energy will take decades to the fact that security of oil supplies will remain a long term problem. Here was a perception not only about declining US oil and natural gas production but longer scarcity of global oil reserves as well. Public concern about global warming was strong and needed to be addressed by the United States.

From the outset, President Obama had a green agenda. He was convinced that the US had to take a leading role in the global energy transition away from fossil fuel to renewable energy.

Not only did the future US outlook for oil and gas production look grim at the time he took office, the President elect believed that if the US were to succeed in taking the leadership in the move to a new clean energy economy, the nation would lead the 21st century global economy.

In order to achieve his goal of creating a new clean energy economy, his energy agenda in 2008 focused on reducing oil imports and fossil fuel use in general, promote renewable energy through tax credits and direct subsidies, enhance energy security and take a leading role towards a global agreement on CO^2 emissions. To achieve these goals all energy and environment agencies in the US government were to be staffed with strong advocates of clean energy and environment.

The Great Recession (Dec 2007- January 2009) enabled the President to allocate $80 billion for the development of renewable energy sources and to improve energy efficiency in all sectors of the economy. It helped create jobs and led to an expansion of solar and wind power until the special program ran out of funds. The Administration failed to get a cap-and-trade bill to cut CO^2 emissions passed in the House of

Representatives but made a commitment to cut such emissions by 17% in 2020 at the Copenhagen Summit.

In the meantime, it had become apparent that less than two years into the first Obama Administration the oil and gas industry without help from the Administration had achieved major successes in economically producing shale gas and tight oil mostly on private land where no Federal government permits were required. Government as well as industry projections had turned very optimistic about continued tight oil and shale gas production growth. Instead of pre-2008 assessments calling for major imports of LNG into the US and a continued surge in oil imports, natural gas imports began to decline and facilities built to export LNG in the future. Oil imports began to decline due to stagnant demand and an increase in tight oil production of almost 4 million b/d (larger than the entire oil production of either Iran or Iraq) between 2008 and 2014.

The Administration's original perception of growing energy scarcity during President Obama's first term in office has almost been reversed entirely when the President entered into his second term in January 2014. President Obama's energy policy evolved from an aggressive pursuit of an environmentally inspired energy policy to a somewhat more pragmatic adoption to the realities of emerging oil and gas markets in the US. The Obama Administration remained opposed to hydrocarbon fuel but slowly began to accept the shale gas production explosion as a bridge fuel to alternative green fuels. The abundance of low cost shale gas enabled the President to act strongly against older polluting coal fired power. Since the sun does not always shine and the wind does not always blow, natural gas is now seen as an intermediate supplementary source of fuel until better batteries will be able to store wind and solar energy.

The Current Situation

The domestic energy situation in the US has dramatically changed since the first year of the Obama Administration. Net crude oil and product imports have been halved between 2007 and 2014 to about 5 million b/d and continue to decline. As for natural gas imports, net LNG and pipeline gas imports are down by almost two thirds since 2007. President Obama can claim that during his tenure in office US dependence on imported oil and natural gas has been reduced significantly but it is largely due to the private sector operating on private and not Federal lands. Obama's biggest contribution has perhaps been the passing of new CAFÉ standards which are already having an impact on automobile efficiency and will continue to reduce gasoline consumption in the US for many years to come. A combination of initially market forces and later EPA implementation of the Clean Air Act, has reduced US CO^2 emissions, a trend which is expected to continue. The Administration expects to play a leading role at the Paris Climate Conference in 2015

The success in reducing US oil imports by about 50% since 2008 has had a positive impact on global oil prices. There is little doubt that without the increase in US oil production oil prices would have been higher in recent years. Geographically, the decline in US oil and other liquids imports has not been spread evenly. The biggest decline (about 50%) was from non-OPEC countries. Oil imports from OPEC producers including the Persian Gulf countries are down by about 40% and imports from Saudi Arabia have declined by only 13% between 2008 and 2013. The main reason for the differences between the Persian Gulf countries and for example Nigeria and North Africa, is related to the gravity and sulfur content of crude oil. The incremental US crude oil production is light and sweet oil, replacing similar oil from OPEC and non-OPEC countries. The Persian Gulf countries produce a heavier and sourer crude oil which is a desirable crude oil for sophisticated upgrading refineries in Texas. In addition, Saudi Arabia is the part owner of the Motiva refinery in the US with a capacity of 600,000 b/d. These refineries use primarily Saudi crude oil. In August of 2014, net crude oil and product imports from Canada are now almost one third higher than net crude oil and product imports from the Middle East.

Recent Energy Outlook of the Obama Administration

US production of tight oil and conventional oil from the Gulf of Mexico is expected to continue for several more years, further reducing US net crude oil imports (net imports because the US may eventually export light sweet oil and import more heavier and sourer barrels). It should be noted, however, that since the summer of 2014, oil prices have dropped sharply. It is not yet clear what will happen to US tight oil production after 2014 if the current or lower oil prices were to prevail for several years. While most oil analysts are cautiously optimistic that at $80 a barrel, US tight oil production will continue to increase albeit at a slower pace in the near future, a slowdown in production growth or temporary stagnation until oil prices increase again cannot be excluded. In case of a sustained oil price significantly below $70 a barrel, investment in non-conventional oil and gas will decline, followed by stagnant and declining oil and natural gas production.

Lower oil prices will also impact the production of Canadian non-conventional oil most of which is exported to the United States. The Administration can positively impact the growth in offshore oil and gas development by making more offshore tracks on Federal land available to the industry. While most tight oil and shale gas production today comes from private properties, the Government can make more Federal lands accessible to the oil and gas industry available to the industry and minimize interference at the Federal level with those developments of oil and gas on private lands. Many in the industry believe that local objections to fracking may lead to additional Federal government regulations.

While at $80 a barrel tight oil production is expected to grow for several more years, long term production sustainability is more uncertain. Many analysts agree with the reference case of the Energy Information Administration (US Department of Energy) that tight oil production will reach a plateau later in the decade or early into the next decade, followed by declining production later in that decade. Optimists, however, believe that new technologies and higher prices may extend production growth well beyond the 2020s.

Due to an imbalance between light sweet oil (US tight oil) and sourer and heavier oil (among others from the Middle East), the US will continue to import some oil from the Middle East and, if the current oil export ban is lifted, export light sweet oil. Net oil imports, however, are expected to continue to fall at least through the early part of the next decade if oil prices remain over $ 70 a barrel. If the lower range of US tight oil resources proves to be correct, it is possible that US oil imports from the Middle East could rise again from the mid-2020s onward.

The natural gas picture is more optimistic in the sense that the known resource base is higher.

Natural gas is currently demand constrained in the US but future domestic demand growth and LNG exports will push volume up significantly. Initially, the Obama Administration was at best lukewarm towards LNG exports but geopolitical developments in Ukraine have helped change the government's attitude in favor of significant LNG exports in particular to Asia and Europe.

The US and Europe receive about 20% of their oil imports from the Middle East. About half of Europe's imports come from the former Soviet Union. With US net oil imports continuing to decline and imports from Canada projected to rise further, the US will be least exposed to oil supply disruption. In contrast, Asia (not including Middle East) now relies for half of its oil imports on the Middle East. Two thirds of Middle East oil exports are now destined for Asia. This trend and the overall growth in merchandise trade between the Middle East oil producers and Asia is expected to grow further.

Impact of US Near Self Sufficiency in Oil and Gas on Middle East Policy

In 1979/80 when oil supply security issues were at the top of the OECD's economic agenda, close to two thirds of Middle East oil was destined for the Americas and Europe and about one third to Asia. In 2013 the roles were reversed and only about 20% of Middle East oil exports went to the Americas and Europe and two thirds to Asian markets. By the end of the decade Asia's share of Middle East oil exports is expected to grow to about 80%. Middle Eastern oil producing countries in return are also buying more Asian goods and services, expanding overall trade between Asian countries and the Middle East. Asia has become the most important market for the Middle East oil producing countries.

Despite the reduced US dependence on Middle East oil and the rising dependence of all major Asian economies on Middle East oil and gas, the United States has remained largely responsible for the defense of the region against external enemies and the supply lines from the Gulf States to the North American European and Asian markets. The cost of the first Gulf War, the Afghan war, the Iraq invasion and more recently the fight against Al Qaida in Yemen and against ISIS in Iraq and Syria was and is born largely by the American taxpayer. The Iraq and Afghan wars together have been costly in terms of casualties and landed the US taxpayer with an additional debt of some three trillion dollars.

The US is unlikely to withdraw from the Middle East in the foreseeable future because of multiple interests in the region. Security of oil and gas supplies is among the most important reasons for the US military presence in the Middle East. After all, one third of world oil exports come from the Middle East. The US may be in the process of further reducing its oil imports in the years to come but allies and partners in Europe and Asia will remain dependent on Middle East oil. A major supply disruption could push oil prices up sharply as happened twice in the 1970s and several times in the past three decades. The US economy along with those of its allies and friends could enter into another major recession in the event of a major oil supply disruption. There is currently no substitute for the US military presence in the Persian Gulf. Neither China nor India have the forward military capabilities and blue water navy required to replace the US military in the region and neither has an interest to build up such a presence at this time. The armed forces of the GCC member states are not integrated and all are dependent on US military capabilities.

There are reasons other than oil supply security for the US continued military presence in the region. A sudden withdrawal of US forces would create a strategic vacuum which could be filled by other powers hostile to the interests of the US and its regional allies. US traditional allies in the GCC would be overwhelmed by Iranian military superiority if the US were to withdraw its 5th fleet and military basis in GCC countries.

Obama Legacy in Energy Policy

The shale gas and tight oil revolution, which was entirely engineered by the private sector since the middle of the previous decade has strengthened the US economy, the balance of trade, a vital part of the energy economy and in the process created 3 million jobs. Government and private sector studies project that with oil prices of around $80 a barrel (currently around $50 in mid-January 2015) tight oil production growth will continue at least until the end of the decade. Opinions differ on production sustainability into the next decade. Hence, net oil imports are likely to decline further in the years to come but could possibly rise again sometime in the next decade. Shale gas resources are more plentiful and production growth is very likely to extend for another two decades. The US is expected to become a net exporter of natural gas (pipeline gas to Mexico and LNG overseas).

If under pressure of a Republican Congress next year, the US government approves a proposed pipeline taking Canadian crude from oil sands to the State of Texas where refineries can profitably turn Canadian heavy oil into light products, an additional million b/d of Canadian oil exports could enter the United States. Additional Canadian oil exports could further reduce the demand for oil imports from outside North America. Allowing the Keystone XL pipeline to be built would create jobs during the construction phase but, more importantly about 90% of the revenues earned by Canada would return to the US in the form of products and services bought by Canada in the US. The environment lobbies have succeeded in blocking the approval of the pipeline and a recent vote in the Democratic controlled Congress did not reach the required veto-proof majority. No action on the Keystone XL pipeline is now expected until sometime in 2015 when the Republican Party will control both houses of Congress.

The rapid growth in non -conventional oil and gas has enhanced US oil and gas supply security. US oil imports have been halved in the past decades and are likely to fall further. In comparison with Europe and in particular East and South Asia which is becoming increasingly oil and gas import dependent, US energy security will be assured for many years to come. The US can use this time to further improve on energy efficiency and development of renewable energy sources. The US will also become a net exporter of natural gas within the next few years. Progress made in the past decade has already reduced natural gas imports to less than 5% of consumption and before the end of the decade the industry expects the US to be strengthening its net exports. This has already had a strong positive impact on natural gas prices in Asia and Europe since close to half of Qatari gas exports originally destined for export to the US, was diverted to Asian markets and some to Europe. The availability of these additional Qatari LNG exports for Asian markets saved the day in Japan after the Fukushima accident. Firmly committed US LNG exports from late 2015 have already had an impact on reducing natural gas pricing in Asia and Europe. In support of these developments, the second Obama Administration has strongly encouraged natural gas exports (LNG) to Europe and Asia. The Ukraine conflict has further strengthened US government resolve to encourage LNG exports to Europe and Asian markets. In the coming year the President with support of a Republican Congress could lift the existing crude oil export ban, enabling excess light oil to be sold abroad.

The Obama Administration's major contribution to domestic energy security since he took office in January of 2009 has been tougher efficiency standards for cars and trucks. They can take credit for not over-regulating non-conventional oil and gas developments. The Administration has taken advantage of the promising new natural gas supplies by implementing strict CO^2 emission standards for electric utilities, leading to a drop in US coal consumption in favor of renewable energy and natural gas.

Obama can claim that during his Administration, US oil consumption peaked, CO^2 emissions declined and both oil and natural gas production returned to a level not seen in decades. In the last two years of the second Obama Administration, the President is committed to reduce CO^2 emissions largely by using existing clean air regulations to close old coal fired power plants. The incoming Republican Majority leader Mitch McConnell (R Kentucky) is expected to fight this policy using budget reviews to delay EPA actions against coal fired power plants.

Will a less oil import dependent US withdraw from the Middle East, a region which produces one third of global oil output and the best hope for growth in conventional oil production? Since 2011 the region's vulnerability to supply disruptions has grown from Libya to Yemen and Iraq. Two thirds of Middle East oil is currently exported to East, South-East and South Asia, including US allies Japan and South Korea. No other country than the US has the naval capabilities to defend the supplies line in the Arab Gulf and the Indian Ocean. The current engagement of the US in the battle against

ISIS, a long term commitment according to President Obama is an indicator that the US remains fully engaged in the Middle East.

The outcome of the struggle against ISIS is highly uncertain and a positive outcome is by no means assured. The outcome of the struggle and the future of US-Iranian bilateral relations will have a major impact on medium to long term oil supply security.

Dr Herman Franssen is the Executive Director of the Energy Intelligence Group. He is a former Chief Economist of the International Energy Agency, Paris. This paper was first written for a Middle East Institute project related to President Obama's policies on the Middle East and included as a part of an MEI report.

CHAPTER FOUR
China's Energy Dynamics
Andrew Leung

Recent Energy Deals with Russia

The supply for China's May 2014 deal with Russia is to come from undeveloped gas fields in Eastern Siberia requiring substantial infrastructure. The Crimea crisis gave China the leverage in having preferential prices agreed. Under a second deal during the APEC Summit, gas is to come from mature fields in Western Siberia supplying Europe. Prices have not been fully agreed but are likely to be even more in China's favour as gas prices have plummeted and the Russian rouble is tumbling due to Western sanctions.

While Russia supplies a quarter (160 bcm) of Europe's gas needs, these deals by no means signal China's energy dependence on Russia. They only add up to 17% of China's total gas needs by 2020. During this period, gas represents 10% of China's energy mix, of which the two deals come to 1.7%.

Above all, these deals do not mean that Russia and China are forming an Eastern bloc against the West. Balancing against US dominance notwithstanding, the world has become so interconnected and interdependent that rigid blocs no longer work. What is more, Russia and China are by no means all-weather friends. Russia's sparsely-populated east is exposed to the influence of Chinese settlements and trade. The history of its Tsarist annexation from the Middle Kingdom remains vivid in the minds of both countries.

Energy Dynamics of Climate Change

China is alive to threats to regime stability posed by energy supply and transit security. This informs China's proactive development of overland pipelines through Central Asia and global energy footprints. It also partly explains China's more assertive stance in the East and South China Seas.

However, over-dependence on energy undermines economic and social sustainability. Overcoming the 'middle-income trap' necessitates more balanced and higher-quality development. Hence reduction of energy intensity repeatedly features in recent five-year plans.

At the APEC Summit, China undertook to cap carbon emissions by 2030. China's confidence in this target is founded on reasonably solid grounds.

According to PEW Charitable Trusts,[1] China became the global leader in wind energy in 2013. China announced in May that over 100 GW of wind energy capacity will be installed to power 100 million households by 2020. With current wind energy cost at 0.4 RMB (US$0.059) per kilowatt-hour, wind energy could displace 23% of China's coal-generated electricity, equivalent to 0.62 gigatonnes (9.4%) of CO^2 emissions.[2]

In 2013, China became the world's largest investor in solar energy with projects worth $22.6 billion with the aim of reaching 50 GW by 2020. According to the Worldwatch Institute, Washington DC, China has 30 million solar households, representing 60% of world's installed capacity.

Hydro-electric power under the five-year plan 2011-2015 is to increase from 220 GW to 290 GW. By end 2013, capacity had already reached 280 GW, equivalent to 22% of China's power capacity.

As for nuclear energy, in addition to 21 existing reactors, 28 more are under construction. Two new plants are to be added annually for the next 15 years. Capacity is expected to increase ten-fold to 400 GW by 2050.

The National Development Reform Commission plans renewable energy to account for 20% of electricity generation by 2020. According to a Chinese Academy of Sciences roadmap to 2050, fossil energy is to decrease from 92.7% of total supply in 2007 to 45%; new and renewable energies to grow from 9% in 2012 to 45%, while nuclear energy is to increase from 1.8% in 2003 to 10%.

By comparison with coal and oil, gas is respectively 43% and 30% less in CO^2 emissions. According to the International Energy Agency (IEA), China is embracing the global 'Golden Age of Gas', representing half the increase in global demand for the rest of the decade, through both home production and imports.[3]

---

1 (http://www.pewtrusts.org/en/research-and-analysis/reports/2014/04/03/whos-winning-the-clean-energy-race-2013 (accessed on 14 November 2014).

2 An estimate by the Worldwatch Institute, 5 January, 2014.

3 As noted in 'China gases up for a New Golden Age' by Keith Johnson in Foreign Policy, 10 June 2014, http://www.foreignpolicy.com/articles/2014/06/10/china_gasses_up_for_a_new_golden_age (accessed on 10 June 2014).

IEA estimates that China has 1,275 TCF (trillion cubic feet) of technically recoverable shale gas reserve, compared with 862 TCF in the US. However, China's reserve is in much more difficult topography. Moreover, existing hydraulic fracturing technologies are less advanced in China, are highly water-intensive and subject to aquifer contamination risks. In any case, shale gas may serve as a bridging lower-emission fuel only if supported by low-carbon technologies, pricing and tax policies, and the highest social and environmental safeguards. [4]

The United States has indicated willingness to share advanced shale technologies and the Chinese government is introducing subsidies for shale gas production. Nevertheless, China remains cautious in exploiting shale gas reserves, lest renewable energy targets may be side-lined, let alone problems of water scarcity and soil and air pollution.

China's urban air pollution has become so serious that an Action Plan[5] was issued by the State Council in September last year. This holds local and regional governments to account for emission targets, clean-energy restructuring, industrial upgrading, energy-saving, and environmental protection. Included also is a program to switch all vehicles to 'fifth-generation' models by 2017 with much higher emission specifications. China is in the race to develop cars of the future, in addition to reducing private vehicle usage through better public transit systems and intelligent cities.

According to the Chinese Academy of Social Sciences (CASS)[6] China will be building some 200 eco-cities in coming years, covering 80% of all prefectures. Many are to be linked by high-speed rail and smart power grids to capture the full potential of irregular natural energies. In 2013, China spent more on smart grids than the US, with $4.3 billion invested, accounting for almost a third of the world's total.[7]

China is expected to attain 70% urbanization rate by 2030. In April 2013, President Xi invoked a vision of 'Ecological Civilization' for a 'Beautiful China' through good

---

4   Golden Rules for a Golden Age of Gas 'Special Report on Unconventional Gas', World Energy Outlook 2012, International Energy Agency http://www.worldenergyoutlook.org/media/weowebsite/2012/goldenrules/WEO2012_GoldenRulesReport.pdf (accessed on 15 November 2014).

5   Action Plan on Prevention and Control of Air Pollution, State Council, September 2013 http://english.mep.gov.cn/News_service/infocus/201309/t20130924_260707.htm (accessed on 15 November 2014).

6   Ecological City Green Book, Chinese Academy of Social Science 2013.

7   China beats US on smart-grid spending for first time, Bloomberg, 19 February, 2014.http://www.bloomberg.com/news/2014-02-18/china-spends-more-on-energy-efficiency-than-u-s-for-first-time.html (accessed on15 November 2014).

quality, efficient, and low-carbon development. A joint report[8] by CASS and the United Nations Development Program (UNDP) explored how this vision may be realized through building sustainable and liveable cities.

All in all, the ambitious pudding remains to be tested. With a fifth of the world's population, how well China manages energy dynamics is likely to define not only her future, for better or for worse, but also her relations with other countries and with Planet Earth.

Andrew Leung is an international and independent China specialist; 40 years in commerce, industry, banking, finance and diplomacy; Helped set up Standard Chartered Asia Ltd ("merchant banking" subsidiary in 1982-83); Twice sponsored by US Government for month-long visits, including a month-long briefing in 1990 for Fortune 50 Chairmen and CEOs on China beyond Tiananmen; Regular TV interviews worldwide; Consultancy to McCreight and Company Inc. on Lenovo's cultural integration with IBM; Editor-at-large for an MEC International consultancy on China's energies; Registered Expert with Thomas Reuters; Gerson Lehrman Group Council Member; Member, Royal Society for Asian Affairs; Brain Trust, Evian Group, Switzerland; Senior Analyst, Wikistrat; Governing Council, King's College London (2004-10); China Futures Fellow, Berkshire Publishing Group, Massachusetts, USA (2011-13); Visiting Professor, London Metropolitan University Business School; Silver Bauhinia Star (SBS), Hong Kong, 2005.

---

8   China National Human Development Report 2013, Sustainable and Liveable Cities, Towards Ecological Civilization, UNDP China and Institute for Urban and Environmental Studies, Chinese Academy of Social Sciences, August 2013 http://www.cn.undp.org/content/dam/china/docs/Publications/UNDP-CH_2013%20NHDR_EN.pdf (accessed on 15 November, 2014)

CHAPTER FIVE
Japan and Asia – Ways Forward
Tatsuo Masuda

Japan's Energy Pathway and its Role in Asia

Japan is the third largest economy and the fifth largest energy consumer, where energy policy matters to sustain its huge economic activities. An excellent track record of energy performance driven by the inherent energy scarcity has lost its sparkles after the Fukushima nuclear disaster of March 2011. The loss of nuclear as quasi-indigenous energy, one of the major pillars of energy supply, is working as a fatal blow to energy policymaking.

The Strategic Energy Plan issued by the government in April 2014 was way short of specifying a concrete energy mix target of the future. And even today, three years and eight months after Fukushima, politicians and the government have failed to do so. The difficulty faced with them is understandable due to the negative public perception of nuclear and increasingly complex requirements for energy policy.

Japan's Energy Policy History

1. Responding to the oil crises (1970s-'80s)
     1973 First oil shock
     1979 Second oil shock
2. Promoting regulatory reform (since 1990s)
3. Coping with global warming issues (since 1990s)
     1997 Kyoto Protocol adopted
     2005 Kyoto Protocol came into effect
4. Enhancing resource security (2000s)
5. Strategic Energy Plan
     2002 Basic Act on Energy Policy enacted
     2003 Strategic Energy Plan established (revised in 2007 & 2010)

6. New Strategic Energy Plan (April 2014) covering:

Safety	Energy Security	Economic Efficiency
Environment	Global Viewpoint	Economic Growth

(Source: METI)

Indeed, the requirements for energy policy have become far more complex as seen above. However, it will be irresponsible for policymakers to remain undecided for such a long period shying away from taking a tough decision on energy pathway, leaving climate measures in limbo to the serious disappointment of the global community. They should learn from history when their predecessors took tough decisions in times of overwhelming uncertainties.

Another challenge for Japan's energy pathway will come after the legal unbundling of the power sector planned from 2018 to 2020. There has been no fundamental change to the Japanese power sector since its basic structure was formed in 1951 allowing regional monopoly by nine vertically-integrated utility companies headed by TEPCO. The outright liberalization of the power sector will offer enormous business opportunities as well as uncertainties.

While Japan is obsessed with its own energy future, a geo-economic mega trend is affecting the global energy and climate future. Around 60% of the global increment of energy demand up to 2040 will take place in Asia (source: IEEJ Asia/World Energy Outlook 2014). The environmental implication is frightening as fossil fuels account for around 84% of the current Total Primary Energy Supply in Asia, which could remain as high as 81% in 2040.

As shown below, Asia will be the 'problem center' of the world if it may fail to effectively address this challenge, but, if successful, it will become the 'solution center' to serve a global well-being.

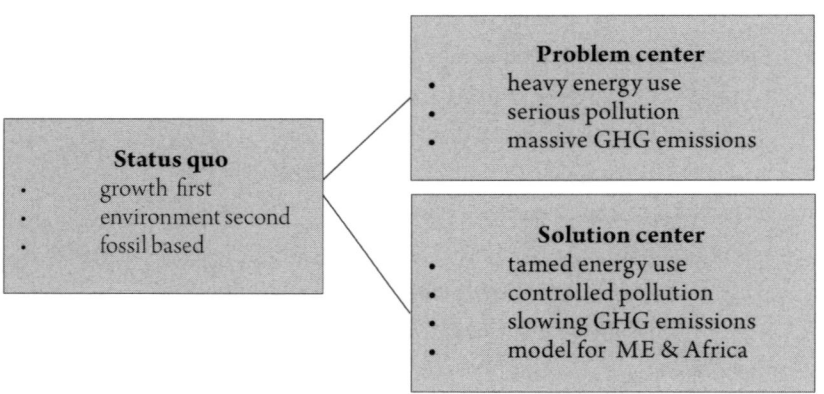

Asian Energy/Climate Scenario

The Sino-US agreement on climate change in November has sent a powerful message to the world as those two alone account for some 42% of the global CO^2 emissions today, which momentum should not be lost by all means. In this regard, what is needed now is the declaration of powerful climate initiative by Japan. By doing so, Japan could give peer pressure on China to accelerate her climate initiative. Whatever China will do matters globally due to its sheer size. For Japan, nuclear restarting is one thing, but not everything. There must be a lot of room for Japan to contribute to the climate initiative of Asian countries, particularly in technologies and knowhow covering renewables, energy efficiency/conservation, energy production/consumption management, etc.

Japan's policymakers as well as the general public should stop being "inward-looking" and do the best to utilise its huge potential to contribute to the global climate initiative. As one of the most advanced countries in energy-related technologies and knowhow, Japan has the duty to do so. At the same time, by doing so, it will be able to identify its energy pathway, which will serve as a role model for Asian countries.

Professor Tatsuo Matsuda is Professor at the Graduate School of Nagoya University of Commerce and Business. He is a board member of SOC Corporation in Tokyo and the advisory board chairman of Faircourt Capital in London. He was Professor at the Tokyo Institute of Technology and Visiting Professor to Paris – University Dauphine. He was Vice President of Japan National Oil Corporation (JNOC) from 2002 to 2005 after heading the Asia Pacific Energy Research Centre (APERC). From 1996 to 2001 he served in Paris as the International Energy Agency Director responsible for oil markets and oil security, and supervised the production of the IEA Monthly Oil Market Report.

CHAPTER SIX
The Legacy of Fossil Fuels
Ron Oxburgh

Managing the Legacy of Fossil Fuels

There are still many uncertainties in climate science but although understanding may differ in matters of detail there is general agreement that the accumulation of greenhouse gases in the atmosphere from burning fossil fuels is already leading to changes in climate over and above those changes that occur naturally such as the alternation of ice ages and inter-glacial periods.

For this reason most governments now agree – if with different degrees of commitment – that action has to be taken to curb the emissions from fossil fuels and industrial processes. In spite of this agreement the concentration of CO^2, the most important greenhouse gas, in the atmosphere has continued to rise over the last fifty years alongside the explosive growth of the world population. Moreover, emissions have grown half as fast again as population. Not only is more fossil fuel being used because there are more people on the planet, but their average per capita energy use is steadily rising as well. To be sure energy sources such as wind, hydro and solar are on the increase too but increasing overall energy demand means that their proportion in the energy mix has scarcely changed and they still account to little more than 15% of energy consumed.

When governments or journalists talk about managing emissions they often present the problem as one of not increasing the rate of our emissions and 'stabilising' at our present levels. Unfortunately this approach misses the point. If we think of the atmosphere as an enormous filling bathtub and the amount of CO^2 in the atmosphere as the level of the water, 'stabilising emissions' means leaving the water taps running at the same rate and continuing to fill the bath. As far as we can tell our bath is at present over half full, and if emissions continue to rise we have only another fifty years or so to avoid catastrophic changes in climate such as breaking down of the Gulf Stream and disruption of the monsoons, not to mention chaotic conditions for world agriculture.

In spite of best efforts to speed the introduction of more renewable energy, not to mention hydro and nuclear, it is clear that at their present rate of growth they will at best simply slightly delay the overflowing of the bath. To have significant impact on the problem the emissions must not be allowed to enter the atmosphere. This means speeding up work on the suite of technologies known as Carbon Capture and Storage (CCS) that trap greenhouse gas emissions at source whether that be a power station, an oil refinery or a cement works. Present practice is to capture the emissions and then transport them – probably by pipeline – to a place where they can be pumped underground and stored in abandoned oil or gas fields or in saline aquifers. To continue the bathtub analogy this is equivalent to easing out the plug from the plughole sufficiently for the water running out to balance the water flowing in. A power station with CCS provides low carbon energy.

All the basic technologies for CCS are well known to the chemical and petroleum engineering industries and combining them as an operating system at an industrial source of CO^2 is perfectly feasible. Unfortunately at the end of 2014, there is, as far as I know, only one power station in the world that has done this and is operating with full CCS. That is the station at Boundary Dam in Saskatchewan, Canada.

The Canadian project was completed with substantial state support. CCS projects in other parts of the world are less advanced but all depend on state support. And there lies the nub of the problem; at present there is no business case for the private sector to make CCS a high priority and commit to the required heavy investment. The costs of the current technology are substantial not only because of the additional plant needed at the CO^2 source, but also because the gas has to be compressed for transport by pipeline and injection underground, and because a suitable subterranean store has to be developed. The additional energy needed to process the flue gases and to compress them could in the case of a power station amount to increasing the cost of generating electricity by 30%. There is clearly little incentive for any power company to install CCS measures on any of their power plants unless Government deploys one or other of both of the levers at their disposal namely regulation or subsidy. At present there has been too little of either to convince industry to implement CCS with any sense of urgency.

Although the developed world would not welcome CCS costs on the massive scale needed to address the global problem, the costs would probably be manageable, particularly in light of the report of the CCS Cost Reduction Task Force that foresaw significant cost savings as the technology developed. Around 70% of the cost of CCS comes from the present capture process which is both capex and opex intensive. A less expensive process is urgently needed to avoid bubbling the flue gases through a solvent that selectively dissolves CO_2 and then heating the solvent to release the gas.

Although the developed world might absorb the additional costs of CCS, the developed world is not where the main challenge lies. At present around half the GHG emissions come from the developed world and half from non-OECD countries and China. Forward projections show the OECD countries emissions dropping slightly while those from other parts of the world increase. By 2030 it is expected that about one third of the emissions will be due to the OECD, one third to China and one third to the others. It is clearly unrealistic to expect countries that have relatively low standards of living and face major immediate problems of health, water supply and food, to give priority to a problem that has its major impact some decades in the future, the more so when the problem was largely generated by more than a century and half of emissions from members of the OECD.

It follows that not only is there an urgent need to implement CCS widely before the bathtub overflows but also to find a way of doing it affordably. One realistic possibility that will be feasible in some places is to use the captured CO_2 for enhanced oil recovery in ageing oil fields. CO_2 is pumped into the field to displace residual oil and enhance its flow. The CO_2 is then retained underground. CCS done this way pays for itself but the opportunities are rather limited.

An alternative approach now receiving attention is to find ways of using the CO_2 to make useful products. At least one business is making money today by taking commercially produced CO_2 and allowing it to react with solids recovered from urban garbage to make carbonate pellets that can be used to make light building blocks. In principle, making solid carbonate building materials is a process that could be widely developed provided there is a plentiful supply of suitable reactants; much natural rock has a suitable composition, but if it has to be crushed to react with the gas the process is not likely to be economic. Other research is focussed on using the CO_2 to make methanol or graphite. Yet other groups are exploring the possibility of using unseparated flue gas directly for some of these reactions. These efforts come under the general name of CO_2 reuse or CO_2 mineralisation.

Whatever efforts are made to reduce our dependence on fossil fuels they will be around for decades to come and if the bathtub is not to overflow we must somehow immobilise their emissions. CCS can be applied both to coal and gas although coal should have priority insofar as it produces roughly half as much useful energy as for the same emissions. Immobilisation of emissions will become pervasive rapidly only when CO^2 can be turned into a money-making resource rather than a waste that must be managed. Given that most of the emissions growth is likely to come from developing countries, mineralisation of emission gases into building materials would seem particularly appropriate. The volumes of solids produced would be massive.

Without some form of CCS urgently I see no way of preventing the bath from overflowing.

Lord Oxburgh of Liverpool KBE FRS is a graduate of University College, Oxford and Princeton University where he worked on the emerging theory of plate techtonics. At Cambridge he was Head of the Department of Earth Sciences and President of Queen's College. From 1988–93 he was Chief Scientific Adviser to the UK Ministry of Defense and Rector of Imperial College, London from 1993–2000. During 2004-05 he was non-executive Chairman of Shell. He is the honorary president of the Carbon Capture and Storage Association.

POSTSCRIPT

Windsor Castle Annual Consultation 2014

Ian Walker

The theme of the discussions was the impact of shale oil and gas developments on regional energy markets around the world.

The Big Picture

- Global economy remains flat with more crises expected making energy demand hard to predict.
- Middle East turmoil expected to worsen and Ukraine developments add to energy uncertainty.
- China confrontation with Japan and Korea yet another instability factor.
- The previous energy pattern is changing fast and will continue to change.

No Shortages

- New sources of oil and gas continue to be found but price will determine exploitation.
- Biofuels, tight oil, shale and alternative energy adding to mix.
- Gas is the overall winner but coal and oil will continue to be base for global energy.
- US self-sufficiency with potential to export will have big impact around the world.
- European energy demand expected to remain flat.
- Big growth expected to continue in Asian markets.
- Supply disruptions arising from Arab Spring balanced by US shale and other new prospects.
- Need to expect the unexpected – Fukishima, Arab Spring, Ukraine.

Climate Change

- Climate change is happening although the scale of the impact of man is unclear.
- Shale has reduced US import needs but encouraged US coal exports now being burnt in Europe.
- International agreement on carbon reduction not working.
- Adaptation to climate change rather than mitigation increasingly popular with politicians.
- China and US remain biggest carbon emitters while Japan has loosened its target post-tsunami.
- Seeking global agreement on specific sectors may offer most practical route ahead.
- Senior figures in China recognise climate change threat to Himalayas with possibility of terrible floods and drought.
- Crippling smog in Chinese cities may encourage cleaner burn coal technologies.

Emerging Gas Markets

- US is moving to set up a number of gas export facilities.
- Expectation is that growing LNG cargoes will lead to regional spot markets.
- Widening the Panama Canal will allow gas tankers more flexibility and cut costs.
- Such markets could reduce the Pacific premium for gas.
- New technologies are making shale exploitation up to 17 per cent more efficient.

The Americas

- Chemical companies are moving to US attracted by cheap shale feedstock.
- Low domestic US price makes investment in shale difficult threatening new prospects.
- Growing use of gas for transport.
- Opening more Federal land to shale exploration will be an issue for future administrations.
- Shale is seen by politicians as key to rebuilding industrial base and jobs.
- There is a strong "war on coal" green lobby that is making coal unappealing in the US outside the coal-producing areas,
- Mexico and Argentina have two of the world's most promising shale reserves.
- Doubts over Argentine development as Brazil has its own shale and other options.
- Mexico best-placed to use its shale and to import US shale for indigenous use and export.

- Canada has options relating to importing US shale under NAFTA.
- Low cost shale threatens future investment in expensive conventional and coal tar
- developments.

Asia

- China will face increased competition from the US utilising low-cost shale.
- Coal is a major problem as it is providing difficult to diversify supply.
- China is looking at a range of global sources as well as developing nuclear.
- China's shale reserves are big but lack water and efficient technology for exploitation.
- Japan paying heavy price for massive import of gas with nuclear switch-off.
- With large national debt it may have to reactivate its nuclear plants.
- Big challenge to convince public where educated women are biggest critics.
- Promising deep drilling on methane hydrates offer Japan a potential energy source but prices are high and more work is needed on technological development.
- Indonesia has massive coal and shale but shale faces problems.
- Heavy bureaucracy complicates development in an already complicated ownership picture.
- India is the third largest energy consumer heavily dependent on coal and oil with gas catching up.
- India's energy demand continues to grow with some success in energy exploration.
- Shale reserves thought to be sufficient to meet 25 years of India's needs.
- Energy imports will continue to be needed and India is now competing in international markets.

Europe

- The European Union is seeking to impose a one size fits all energy policy.
- Such a policy would be detrimental to Central and East European countries reliant on coal.
- De-industrialisation is a major cause of falls in European carbon production.
- Britain leading the way with incentives to encourage domestic shale exploration.
- Russia remains a major supplier of gas but Ukraine raises energy security issue.
- Ukraine problems illustrate the underlying energy security issues felt by Russia - unhappy at having to rely on Ukraine for much of its European gas exports.

Russia

- Russia facing major problems as Europe reduces demand as it needs less fuel and imports cheap US coal.
- Agreeing big long-term deals with China is proving difficult as Chinese are demanding market prices lower than Russia expects.
- Japan is seen as a more likely long-term partner for Russian energy exports.
- Gazprom's lead role in energy is being supplanted by Rosneft and private sector players.
- Domestic subsidies force Russia to seek profits elsewhere at a time when energy is its main earner.
- Ukraine problems illustrate the underlying energy security issues felt by Russia – unhappy at having to rely on Ukraine for much of its European gas exports.

Middle East

- Uncertainty continues with Libyan output affected and Iraq production slow to rise.
- Egypt has gone from being a gas exporter to the need for major imports.
- Gas finds in the East Med offer some hope as Lebanon moves to encourage offshore exploration.
- Israeli exports of its gas finds will happen – either via Cyprus to Europe or Turkey.
- Politics in the region very complex and will make any development slow.
- Syria illustrates the many factions involved in a civil war involving proxies.
- Iran deal would be significant if Iran is allowed to export its major gas reserves.
- Confirmation of such a deal uncertain and developments would take time.
- Domestic energy subsidies in the Gulf are soaking up energy production and is one of the reasons that nuclear is being examined to allow exports to remain unaffected.

Carbon Storage

- Three full-scale carbon capture projects underway in Canada, England and Scotland.
- One involves the use of oxyfuel that reduces carbon gases but adds to cost.
- Carbon capture will remain expensive but demonstration projects allow technology to be developed and refined for use in heavily polluting countries.

- Coal gasification – burning coal underground to produce gas – may be a practical way of keeping carbon in the ground.

Ian Walker is managing director of MEC International which offers small expert teams of former ambassadors, bankers and business people to deal with a range of business challenges across the Middle East and related regions. He worked with Paul Tempest to establish Windsor Energy Group as a neutral platform for policy-makers and energy practitioners to review changes in global energy markets. He also runs a number of sister organisations that look at how technological innovation is impacting energy players and the challenges facing the development of nuclear power. Ian began as a political journalist in both print and radio before running companies offering expert corporate communications and government relations advice.

CONCLUSIONS
The New Geopolitics of Energy
Avoiding Catastrophe

Paul Tempest

An Acute Danger from the Changing Climate

The most pressing message from this analysis is its warning about the likely severe impact of climate change within the next 35 to 50 years. The accumulation of greenhouse gas in the earth's atmosphere can be attributed largely and with a high degree of certainty to industrialisation in the nineteenth century mainly to the use of coal in Europe and North America and to an acceleration of much wider pollution of the atmosphere during the twentieth century. There has been no sign of abatement so far in the twenty-first century. Indeed, by 2035, global emissions of carbon dioxide are expected to be almost double the level in 1990. We are no longer discussing a hypothetical outcome in a distant future. The build-up of scientific evidence has already reached a tipping point, a very serious matter that should be of immediate concern world-wide.

For the great majority of children on this planet today, the risk may be all too apparent. Within their lifetime, they will most probably witness major economic disruption caused by climate change. Unless a strong curb on greenhouse gases can be devised and achieved, these, our children and grandchildren, are likely to witness a progressive sequence of events including the breaking down of the Gulf Stream, the melting of the icecaps and the disruption of monsoons, each having chaotic impacts on global agriculture, accessibility to clean drinking water and curtailment of food supply. Along that track, rising sea-levels pose very serious problems for the energy industries with considerable damage to specialised ports, power stations, particularly nuclear power plants and liquefied natural gas plants sited close to the shoreline and to exploration and development activity. As a consequence, damaging disruptions to international trade and investment will threaten to slow down the momentum of global economic growth and the relief of poverty and distress.

Fossil Fuels are Necessary to Maintain Growth Momentum

As Lord Oxburgh argues with compelling scientific evidence and a relentless logic (in Chapter 5), we cannot afford to shut off the use of fossil fuels without any credible replacement in sight. Indeed, with continued population growth and enhanced expectations of a steady rise in global per capita income, the demand for coal, gas and oil can be expected to continue to rise roughly in line with population and economic growth. Wind, solar and hydro will continue to grow but will find it very difficult to enhance their small current share of the energy mix, less than 15% at present out of which hydro accounts for half. Nuclear development (4% of the mix) has been slowed markedly by the decisions of Japan and Germany to run down their nuclear capacity and by the widely held fears that rogue terrorists and irresponsible states will seek and may achieve a proliferation of nuclear capacity as a first step on the road to acquiring a nuclear weapon manufacturing capacity of their own. So globally, we have to accelerate much more strongly fundamental research and the rapid implementation of new non-pollutant and less dangerous energy technologies. Meanwhile it is essential that we invest adequately and evenly to ensure an increased supply of fossil fuels to tide us over.

Investment in Carbon Capture and Storage

So our first priority is to ensure that carbon capture and storage (CCS) is implemented worldwide as fast as possible to the point where we can substantially reduce its impact on the atmosphere. This is not an impossible task, but it is one that requires a global consensus on the necessity for this change and a much wider understanding of the dangers that we will otherwise face. The problem at present is essentially one of attracting adequate investment in these new technologies. What is seen at present as a dubious prospect of costly and incomplete waste-management has somehow to be transformed into a positive commercial venture with long-term prospects of generating substantial profit. At the same time governments have to be fully convinced of the urgency of these issues and the need to move to much more effective international co-operation and implementation.

Adverse Impacts of a Falling Oil Price

The abrupt fall in the oil price in late-2014 has diminished both the flow of surplus funds from the fossil-exporters and the appetite of the energy investors seeking a fast, secure stream of profit. Consumer governments worldwide have also become increasingly nervous about their own budget shortfalls and about preserving secure access to imported energy. So many are focussing on the short-term to the neglect of the long-term fundamentals. Investment so far in carbon capture and storage has been very slow indeed with only one plant (in Canada) operating at present and that single plant is dependent on very heavy state subsidy. The high cost of subsidy and consequent low expectations of an acceptable rate of return for the commercial and industrial investor and high risk in mostly brand-new, unproven technology is a strong deterrent for the private sector. Some radical new thinking and a burst of industrial innovation is needed to dispel this gloom.

Reinvigorating the International Infrastructure

In our view, much of the the international infrastructure today is outdated, inefficient and no longer fit for purpose. New institutions, such as a brand-new international energy bank, a new co-ordination agency for stimulating advances towards more efficient energy use and carbon capture and new financing packages will need the backing of a re-focussed United Nations protocol on carbon capture.

Now for the Good News – Ample Fossil Resources

As indicated in Table 2 (page 8), proven coal, oil and natural gas reserves swollen by new discoveries of shales and deep-water oil and gas offer some confidence that supply can meet demand until the bridge to new technology can be safely crossed.

How Do We Achieve These Carbon Capture Objectives?

As a starting point for our Windsor Energy International Consultations in 2015, I offer the matrix outlined in the Prologue of this book.
1. Long-term Objective: we must ensure that the global population and economy is not put at risk by the failure to implement permanent effective climate change remedies in good time.
2. Short-term Objective: the acceleration of new technology and stimuli for the necessary financing must now be seen to be widely on the right track.
3. Resources: ample fossil fuel resources can help to bridge the gap.
4. Intelligence: co-ordination of ever-advancing telecommunications should assist in market transparency and speed of implementation.

5. Obstacles: the greatest obstacles are essentially political – power-block rivalries, regional in-fighting for access to resources, local squabbles over investment failures.
6. Surprise: we somehow have to develop a new means of conveying optimism and confidence in the global long-term future.
7. Superior Technology and Skills: New centres of technical excellence and skills training will need access to both public and private financing and incentives to attract the best recruits.
8. Identifying Weakness: high-lighting weakness is as good a route as any to enhance efficiency. A new generation of energy automation and enhanced co-ordination will be needed to displace the obsolete and atrophied systems still to be found worldwide.
9. Communication Co-ordination: this will be needed to achieve the best results.
10. Simple Orders: the use of a simple, standard world language understood by all is a prerequisite. For the time being, this will be English. Within 50-100 years, it may well be Chinese.
11. Concentration of Fire: new global, regional and national centres will be needed to mobilise the right resources whenever major obstacles are encountered.
12. Reinforcement Options: to what extent can additional resources be called up through the international agencies responsible for such responses?
13. Securing the Ground: what incentives can be devised to curb new pollution?
14. Follow-up: enhanced sensitivity for consequences hitherto unseen.
15. Contingency Planning: separate sessions at the 3-day WEG International Consultations in Windsor Castle in March 2015 will address these issues.

Atmosphere, Oceans and Space – The New Science

Among the advanced scientific community, the penny has again already dropped. A rational scientific consensus was already being expressed 20 years ago, resulting in the Kyoto Conference of 1997 and consequent Kyoto Protocol endorsed by the United Nations but deeply flawed by the division of governmental opinion, the determination of industry and commerce led by the heavy weight of the energy industries to sweep the proposed targets and strategies under the carpet and a confused, largely indifferent response from public opinion. Within the last five years, a new tipping-point has been reached as the leading scientists have realised the gravity of the threat to the earth's atmosphere. The pace of research swollen by access to the necessary funds has provided re-evaluations of the usefulness of ocean, space, chemical and medical research. It is here where we may well find the solutions to some of our current concerns about an abundant long-term global energy supply.

Books and Articles by Paul Tempest

Books

International Energy Options (1981)

International Energy Markets (1982)

Energy Economics in Britain (1983)

The Politics of Middle East Oil (1993)

The Manila Surprise 1762-64 (2002)

An Enduring Friendship (Gulf/UK, 2006)

The Arabists of Shemlan (2006)

The Bank of England – A Thread of Gold (2008)

Envoys to the Arab World (2009)

The Future of the Bank of England (2011)

Greenwich and the London River (2012)

Surviving the Storm – The New Geopolitics of Energy (Medina Publishing, 2015)

Major Articles

Financing the North Sea (BofE 1979)

Gas in the 21st Century (Conant 1985)

OPEC – A View from the Industry (1990)

Russian Oil and Gas (Shell PAE 1990)

Energy Strengths of India (Malaviya 1992)

Petroleum Choices in China (CNPC 1997)

The Problem with Nuclear (GoE 1998)

Improving Oil Market Data (IEA/GoE 2002)

The North Sea 1973-2013 (GoE 2013)

UK Energy Policy (GoE 2013)

Trinidad – A Bright Future (GoE 2014)

ANNEX

THE WINDSOR ENERGY GROUP 2015

Chairman since 2004
Lord (David) Howell of Guildford PC
ex-Secretary of State for Energy and then for Transport, later ex-FCO Minister for the Commonwealth and ex-FCO Minister covering International Energy. President of BIEE 2003-2012

Executive Director since 2009
Ian Walker
Managing Director of WEG 2000-2009

Regional Co-ordinator since 2006
Stephen Nash CMG
ex HBMA in Georgia and Latvia

Scientific Adviser since 2006
Lord (Ronald) Oxburgh of Liverpool
ex-Chairman of Shell

Nuclear Adviser since 2005
Lady (Barbara) Judge
ex-Chair of UKAEA

Diplomatic Adviser since 2000
HE Khaled Al-Duwaisan GCVO
Ambassador of Kuwait and Dean of the UK Diplomatic Corps

Secretary of the International Panel since 2002
Paul Tempest
ex-DG of WPC 1991-99, first Chair of the BIEE and VP 2001-09 and Executive Director of WEG 2000-09

Other Members of the International Panel

Dr Wang Tao (China)
Ex-Minister, ex-President, China National Petroleum Corporation

Dr Subruto (Indonesia)
Ex-Secretary-General of OPEC and ex-Minister of Mines and Energy

Professor Tatsuo Masuda (Japan)
Adviser to Chairman of Japex and ex-Vice-President of JNOC

HE Arne Walther (Norway)
Ambassador to Japan and ex-Ambassador to Austria and India; ex-Secretary-General of International Energy Forum, Riyadh

Mr Mehmet Ogutcu (Turkey)
Ex-Director of International and Corporate Affairs, BG Group (British Gas)

Dr Herman Franssen (United States)
Ex-JChief Economist, International Energy Agency, Paris

Mr Pawel Olechnowiwicz (Poland)
CEO Gruppo Lotos, Gdansk

WINDSOR ENERGY BACKGROUND

The Windsor Energy Group was founded in London in 2000 under the chairmanship of the late Sir David Gore-Booth and with the full support of HE Khaled Al-Duwaisan, Dean of the Diplomatic Corps and Ambassador of Kuwait.

WEG aims to provide a high-level forum to address global, regional and national energy issues and problems arranging briefings, meetings, seminars, private lunches and dinners throughout the year at the request of the London Ambassadors and their Governments. All discussions are conducted on a strictly non-attributable basis to ensure a full and frank exchange of views.

The Group meets annually each March inside Windsor Castle for a three-day Consultation and consideration of the discussions of the previous year and programme for the coming year. Invitations are extended to leading Ambassadors in London and to the 20 or so industry and commercial sponsors to attend the Ambassadors Briefing in the Dungeon, a Reception in the Warden's lodgings, and a Dinner held in the Vicars Hall constructed in 1415 to celebrate victory at the battle of Agincourt. Here in this room Shakespeare acted in and directed the first production of *The Merry Wives of Windsor* before Queen Elizabeth I. An escorted late-night tour of St George's Chapel has also always been included in the programme.

Detailed reports of the WEG Consultations have been produced for participants as follows:

2003 The Long Shadow of Iraq	2009 Impacts of the Financial Crisis
2004 Towards an Energy Breakthrough	2010 Russia Changes Course
2005 A Desperate Need for Co-operation	2011 New Middle East Anxieties
2006 Rising Global Uncertainty	2012 China – A Changing Energy Policy
2007 A Big Shock is Coming	2013 A Year of Snakes and Eagles
2008 Into the Maelstrom	2014 US Shale and Global Gas Prospects